WHAT PEOPLE ARE SAYING ABOUT BRAND INTIMACY

With *Brand Intimacy*, brand experts Rina Plapler and Mario Natarelli unlock a powerful inner truth about brands—that the best ones create intimate, enduring bonds with customers that leads to revenue growth and value. Powerful and insightful, *Brand Intimacy* brings a fresh, new perspective on how to build brands and strengthen customer bonds in today's hyper-connected world. The book blends science, analytics, psychology and research along with simple, practical examples to help brand owners and brands achieve their goals.
  —**Jonathan Bell**, Managing Partner, WANT Branding

We are in a new age. It is critically important to discover how our decisions are made, whether made about brands or our role in society. This book illuminates and quantifies the importance of emotion in the decision process and provides a winning construct to achieve emotional brand intimacy.
  —**John Diefenbach**, Chairman, MBLM, and Former CEO, Landor

MBLM's insights and creativity helped us strengthen our brand and improve the way we connect with consumers.
  —**Giorgio Galli**, Design Director, Timex Group

A must-read that captures the importance of appealing to instincts and emotions to build powerful brands.
  —**Fran Gormley**, Adjunct Associate Professor of Marketing, NYU Stern

A great look at what inspires people to engage with brands and how to use that to your advantage. *Brand Intimacy*, both the book and the concept, is important for marketers to understand and for brands to use wisely.
  —**Sami Main**, Digital Media Reporter, Adweek

Critical reading for any marketer or business leader. *Brand Intimacy* should change how marketers think about everything.

    —**Jill Malandrino**, Global Markets Reporter, Nasdaq

For those looking to grow their brand and their business, *Brand Intimacy* is a must-read. It is a thoughtful examination that questions our current thinking on marketing, while offering a better solution, borne through careful examination and consumer insights.

    —**Hamza Mustafa**, CEO, PCFC Investments

Brand Intimacy is a comprehensive guide to brand building for any modern marketer or business executive.

    —**Richard Rubenstein**, President, Rubenstein PR

This book is amazing and scary. It demonstrates how businesses are run is not how we manage brands. Aligning an organization, prioritizing emotion and thinking of brand relationships like human ones demonstrates a far more compelling approach than most business books espouse.

    —**David Spencer**, Strategic Advisor, Golf in Dubai

BRAND INTIMACY

A NEW PARADIGM IN MARKETING

MARIO NATARELLI
& RINA PLAPLER

Hatherleigh Press is committed to preserving and protecting the natural resources of the earth. Environmentally responsible and sustainable practices are embraced within the company's mission statement.

Visit us at www.hatherleighpress.com and register online for free offers, discounts, special events, and more.

BRAND INTIMACY

Cover and Interior Design by Hui Min Lee
Author photographs by Mike Sheehan

Printed in the United States
10 9 8 7 6 5 4 3 2 1

To Daniel Kahneman, who changed
the way we think about thinking.

CONTENTS

INTRODUCTION

WHY THIS BOOK AND WHY NOW?

After more than two decades branding companies, countries and people around the globe, we have realized that growth, in some shape or form, is at the core of all our clients' needs, and that "brand" could be an extremely effective and powerful tool to facilitate demand. While desire for growth remains constant in today's increasingly interconnected world, the challenges vary. Take political disruption, which can birth populism and an anti-establishment ethos. This creates a polarized population with highly charged views that can affect trade, supply chain optimization and globalization. There's also organic growth: for the past decade, countless companies have optimized costs and stripped down any and all aspects of their businesses to the extreme in order to save costs and maximize profits. But what's next for them? How can they find new growth? We see technology transforming everything we do in our work, at home and at play. Companies face fast-paced cycles of innovation with steep opportunity costs and profound risks that can render them extinct—quickly. Last, demographics are shifting and with them, the familiar associations and behaviors of now-aging boomers are changing. A new demographic is emerging—millennials, an entirely different generation who require new understanding to effectively reach.

What can businesses do to advance? And what role does brand play?

Brand can be a key asset in framing opportunities; however, it requires thinking about brand in a different way than traditional marketers or business schools suggest. It requires a new paradigm designed for today's times.

How did we arrive at this new way of thinking? We spent nearly a decade conducting qualitative and quantitative research with more than 12,000 consumers in the U.S., Germany, Japan, Mexico and the UAE. We fielded and interpreted over 20,000 qualitative brand stories that comprised 2,000 pages of verbatim responses explaining how individuals form relationships with brands. We turned to quantitative research and, over the course of several years, analyzed 100,000 brand evaluations. Through factor analysis and structural equation modeling, we were able to better understand which levers need to be pulled to build bonds between brand and consumers. We built a data engine to compute, compare and dynamically render rankings, head to head comparisons and detailed brand scores. We have applied our new paradigm to create brands and to reignite established ones. Each year, since 2015, we publish an annual study on intimate brands and their impact.

But let's take a step back.

We are all shaped by brands, whether we realize it or not.

The process starts in life with toy trucks and princesses and only continues as we age. The cars we drive; the household items we prefer; the food we eat; the clothes we wear; the places we travel; the sports teams we follow; the celebrities we admire; the companies we trust; the politicians we elect—while the average person may not think about these as brand choices, marketers have spent decades working hard to create perceptions and the associations that make us want to try or purchase one brand over another.

Whenever we ask people to share with us the brands they are intimate with, many times they will initially respond with, "None." But then you start asking them about their car, their camera, their phone, their sneakers, their favorite drink…and all of a sudden, they discover themselves to in fact be passionate advocates for brands they favor.

In other words, we are more attached to brands than we realize.

That is because brands are much more than a name, a logo, or a jingle. Yes, they are business assets that create value for the companies that represent them; and yes, they can be products, services, people, and places; and *yes*, they can drive demand, command price premiums and increase loyalty. But they're more than that; or at least they have the *potential* to be more than that.

So, with so many books out there already that talk about branding, why another one?

It's simple. We have found that approaches to branding have largely stagnated. Most feature models, structures, and thinking from *decades* ago. Those ideas were leading and advanced in their day, to be sure; but too many things have changed for these approaches to be *relevant,* much less cutting edge. Think about it: practically speaking, could you use a computer from the 1980s today? You could probably still benefit from its functionality; however, it would be very limited in what it could do. It would not align with any new software, nor sync with your other devices, and you'd likely have some compatibility problems when sharing files. It is essentially the same principle with marketing. Why use yesterday's thinking for today's (or tomorrow's) challenges?

We now know, without a shadow of a doubt, that people make decisions and process information based on emotion and intuition.

That is relatively new information, which comes from advancements in neuro-science and behavioral science. It's a far cry from prevailing sentiment that defines us as thoughtful, rational beings; yet most marketers and business leaders have neglected this insight, and continue to ignore the most powerful component of brand building and growth: *emotion*. Rather, most continue to overestimate the importance of rational, hierarchical-based thinking, founded on what we now know are faulty decision making constructs. In essence, they are misdiagnosing the marketplace and, as a result, are providing the wrong cures.

And we wonder why results don't change.

As big a topic as emotion is, decision makers are slow to change. The proven and established is safe; the new and daring, a bit more precarious.

So, yes—another book about brand, but not *just* another book. A book for winning in the marketplace of today. One based on very different thinking. One that represents a new paradigm. One that is dedicated to building bonds with customers. One that translates the academic perspective of intimacy into an instructive and inspiring marketing model for building successful brands. One that is proven to increase growth and profitability.

Welcome to the new world of brand intimacy.

1

CONTEXT & UNDER- STANDING

An overview of early inspiration, the evolving marketing landscape, existing branding approaches and initial qualitative findings. Here we outline why yesterday's thinking is not designed for the present and why brands must change.

1-1

THE POWER OF BRANDS

We believe in the power of brands. The power to inspire, align, and endure. But we've also witnessed many that fall short, miss the mark, or simply fade away. As partners and practitioners, we've been building brands for decades across geographies, industries, and organizations of varying types and sizes. Along the way, we've continually searched for fundamental truths about what makes a brand successful, compelling, and memorable.

At their core, we believe brands are best described as a relationship—a bond, built on values, beliefs, associations and performance. And, like any human relationship, brands are complex, dynamic, and often hard to manage or bend to your will. This is a vastly different way to conceptualize this highly abstract thing called a brand. The term itself—"brand"—has been distorted to mean everything from a name or logo to your reputation or a company's outbound message or campaign. Though all of these components are integral to a brand, focusing more on the bonds created versus the inert representations is a pivotal new consideration.

The practice of leveraging brands to promote or sell products and services has for decades treated brands in a very static way. There is a tendency to use more rational and pragmatic methods to create, measure and manage them, which seems at odds with the very emotional nature of what attracts us in the first place. Over time, we began to suspect that there had to be a better way to understand, shape and manage brands. This thinking has led us on a two-decade long journey, drawing from the many lessons we've learned from the brands we've played a role in creating and also those we admire from afar.

Together with our partners at MBLM, we've witnessed the evolution of branding through the decades, and have had the privilege of building and shaping some of the most reputable brands in the world. Through each decade we've summarized the seismic forces that were shaping brands in fundamental and profound ways.

In the 80's, the very notion of brands as assets to be leveraged gained prominence with major (mostly Western) companies. Fueled by mergers and acquisitions and companies' expanding footprints, in the 90's brands became increasingly globalized, crossing borders, cultures and demographics.

In the 00's, the internet revolution began its digital impact on all things marketing and brand related. The phrase "from bricks to clicks" sums up the fervor to imbue brands with digital relevance. In the 10's, technology continued to drive innovation and breakthroughs for brands. Data, advanced algorithms, social media and mobile adoption are just some of the forces that have made brands more enabled and more pervasive than ever before.

We believe there is still a new next stage of transformation for brands; however, before we go there, let's take a more detailed look at some compelling brand transformation milestones through the years. We've selected these examples to illustrate the power and potential in brands. These will also help chart the course of our experience in shaping brands to solve significant business challenges. Most of these cases are from the 2000s and involved solving unique global brand issues, often utilizing digital as a key element. This book features the learnings we have since codified into methodologies for every brand we've helped grow. In examining the hundreds of brands we've built across categories and geographies, we've narrowed it down to sharing six specific brands and the lessons gained.

TRANSFORMATION AND RENEWAL

UPS

Perhaps the clearest and most compelling examples that showcase the power of brands occur when a business has an opportunity for growth or expansion, and their brand is able to lead the way. In these cases, the brand has to shed its skin and be reborn in order to become different and stronger. To transform and renew, the brand must equip itself to be able to build numerous new bonds with employees, partners, customers, and consumers. When this occurs in a large organization, the challenge is massive and the process is complex, often taking many years and a profound commitment.

A vivid example of brand transformation on a grand scale was participating in the comprehensive rebranding of UPS, a century-old company, which at the time was looking to expand its focus, presence, and impact. From its founding in 1907 as a retail merchandise delivery service in Seattle (using the pullman brown color on its vans to denote first class service) to earning its reputation as America's most reliable package delivery service, UPS had become a global logistics company specialized in the movement of goods, information and funds. To bridge the perception gap, the UPS brand needed to be reimagined.

At the time, the brand highlighted the company's history; now, it needed to be able to help herald its future.

1920s   1937   1961   2003

UPS brand identity transformation

Various UPS touchpoints following the rebranding

Claude Salzberger, our partner and president of MBLM, describes the work he led that spanned several years: "At the core of the process, at the end of all the research, interviews, and analysis, we developed two important components: a powerful brand strategy and an effective visual identity. The first informed the latter and together these reflected the potential for the business. We managed to translate a powerful business idea and express it through a new brand that was poised for success. We essentially took their strengths and we elevated them higher."

"Synchronizing the world of commerce" became the shorthand for a detailed new brand positioning initiative. This strategy both grounded the transformation and set the compass for where the company was navigating. From this platform, and with a clearly articulated vision in hand, the rebranding efforts became visually dynamic and bold. Colors were carefully selected, grid features designed and icons created to demonstrate and complement the idea of synchronized commerce. The UPS story is one of transformation and renewal on a massive scale. The challenge spanned more than 350,000 employees, the ninth largest airline fleet and every vehicle, the uniform, and package…this story could be a book of its own!

Against the context of this complex rebranding effort, one lesson that served us well is that the power of a focused brand strategy and design can, when done right, align and accelerate business transformation on a massive scale. With UPS, we see the perfect example of how brands lead businesses; they don't trail behind them. Brands have to both reflect the ideal of the future and deliver in the present. Too often, brands are designed for and boxed in by the current state. Though seemingly prudent, this tends to undermine the potential brands have to inspire employees and partners, and it limits their opportunities to innovate and grow.

INTEL

The challenge of the Intel rebranding involved the complex relationships sometimes inherent within brands or portfolios, more than any external forces.

The parent/child relationship between corporate and product brands usually requires careful attention.

Intel had created one of the most effective ingredient brands in the world. In PC compatibles, "Intel Inside" was synonymous with Intel-powered computing. This resulted in a portfolio of processor chips well known by partners and manufacturers, and a campaign of strong awareness with consumers. What was lacking was a corporate brand that connected to its products and the Intel Inside campaign. People understood what a Pentium delivered, or how Intel Inside benefited them; yet the nature and values of the company behind these offerings remained vague, visually disconnected, and remote. This was a classic case of the child brand (product or campaigns) overpowering the parent. So, Intel needed to bring the corporate brand back into the picture.

Key to this effort was finding an effective way to link the successful aspects of the Intel Inside campaign with the corporate brand itself, while simultaneously giving the brand a broader purview and a deeper meaning, letting it lead the next generation of technology advancements. And, like UPS, the rebranding set a bold new vision for the company. It absorbed the positive equities of the ingredient campaign, linked to the products in a more meaningful way, and inspired a large ecosystem of stakeholders, including employees, investors, partners, consumers and suppliers.

The lesson learned with Intel is that brands rarely exist in isolation. Often, the power of a brand has to be understood in relation to other brands and their inherent associations. Harnessing a brand fully can only come from

FROM: **TO:**

Before: Intel's corporate brand and Intel Inside logo   After: Intel's updated combined corporate identity

comprehending the complete ecosystem of value created and the role of all the brands at play. Ideally, value is created from the parent down to the children, yet on occasion value goes in the other direction.

AMERICAN AIRLINES

Rebranding American Airlines represented nearly ten years of pursuing, cajoling, and pitching various leaders and executives. After nearly a decade focused on cutting costs, senior management realized that they needed to focus on delivering the best possible customer experience, starting with replacing an aging fleet with 600 new aircraft. This decision opened the door to reinventing the passenger journey from top to bottom. To showcase these important initiatives, American Airlines embarked on a comprehensive re-branding program.

As part of a consortium of companies from the Interpublic Group (a collection of marketing agencies) tasked with the airline's brand revitalization effort, Claude Salzberger was invited to lead the FutureBrand team responsible for the evolution of the airline's 40 year-old corporate identity. Claude notes: "The opportunity for American Airlines was to seize an important moment to re-define a nation's flying experience and opportunity to restore the airline's once proud stature in aviation. Perhaps more than any other industry, airlines present the challenge of having to seamlessly integrate the new brand across a diverse set of channels, touchpoints, and experiences. From planning your trip through to pre-check-in, check-in, in-flight and post flight, the entire customer journey is one continuous, revolving interface with the brand."

As the customer journey has become increasingly enhanced by digital touch-points and channels, online check-ins, mobile apps, check-in kiosks, gate monitors, in-flight entertainment systems, and interfaces, managing the role and expression of the brand is key. Behind these screens are a range of systems, apps, and tools, all driven by disparate technologies, linked to even more sources of data and layers of digital infrastructure. Although the rebranding of physical elements is thought to be more costly and complicated, now the electronic domain presents an even greater transformation challenge.

To that end, the MBLM team worked tirelessly to ensure a consistent user experience that would express the brand personality to the fullest, understanding the effort and importance required to align and bring a new brand to life across its complex digital universe. To reimagine things like the mobile and online social experience, gates, and kiosks, we applied four guiding principles—personalization, consistency, simplicity, and usability. Recognizing the important role that stronger bonds can play, we created modular graphic user interface kits, digital guidelines, and detailed product specifications to enable these principles to scale and ensure a consistent user experience that would express the brand personality to the fullest.

The takeaway here is that the power behind cohesion and a consistent customer experience reaches across all touchpoints, of which digital is the most critical. How people experience a brand at any moment has impact, so ensuring consistent, frictionless engagement is paramount.

New American Airlines branding and digital experience

AMBITION AND SCALE

THE PALM

When a product is the brand, you're generally working with a straightforward relationship, one that determines the connection between what is offered and how you want consumers to feel about it. From bubbles fizzing in your mouth to the smoothness of your shave, product brands have tangible, tactile powers that provide fertile ground in which to anchor a brand.

So imagine the challenge to define a brand when it is the world's largest man-made island still five or more years from completion. The scale and complexity of this ambition was unparalleled, and changed our very understanding of what a brand can do or be—more than a product or a logo, it can be an icon, an inspiration, a community, even a destination.

In the case of The Palm (unnamed at the time), we were presented with something otherworldly, completely off the charts in terms of boldness and uniqueness. Compounding matters was that the development was located in the then little-known emirate of Dubai, in the Arabian Gulf, run by a handful of trusted government employees with no corporate entity and no real estate experience.

The secret of Dubai quickly became clear—visionary leadership. From the ruler, Sheikh Mohammed, to his trio of senior executives could be found the perfect combination of ambition, desire, and the ability to make things happen. With determination, speed, and focus as goals, we had to completely reinvent the very concept of brand building for a scale and pace that was never seen before.

What's more, The Palm project forced us to define what a brand stood for years before it existed in reality, while giving it credibility, confidence, and wonder. "Owning the Eighth Wonder of the World" was our bold positioning for The Palm. The key word here was the first one—own. The Palm represented the first example of freehold property in the emirate, and so we chose to highlight this quality in every aspect of its emerging brand. To complement the strong language was a logo and visual style that was restrained, elegant, and premium.

Materials were produced to portray a statement of professionalism and trust. This was a dream that was going to be made real; this was going to change the world of real estate and travel destinations. We stressed that this was something not just to believe in, but to be a part of.

The scale of this project also necessitated a range of unusual branding needs from naming every street on the island based on local date palm species to a program that branded an airship to deliver VIP experiences to owners and new prospects alike. And when your brand is something that is literally visible from outer space, you try to find every way possible to showcase the view of the product—and, in some cases, lift buyers and prospects, literally flying above the man-made island to appreciate The Palm from the air.

A variety of touchpoints of The Palm

And the work didn't end there. A complete brand foundation was created long before there was even a marketing department or a sales center. We designed renderings and drawings before there were finished plans and defined the language that would create the diverse products that were purchased at record rates and levels from buyers around the world.

The Palm helped put Dubai's right foot forward on the global stage. And it was brand that led the way, for both the product and the business. It truly is a world-class destination of unique appeal and grandeur—a place formed by the vision of a few and a strong brand enjoyed by many and visible from space.

It taught us the importance of being bold and innovative, charting new waters and creating strong bonds with customers, even years in advance of a brand being complete. We learned to try and trial new ways to go to market, to not be afraid to experiment and to truly celebrate ambition and scale.

MEXICO

As if the world's largest man-made island wasn't challenge enough, how about the ambition of an entire country? We were hired to develop a new visual identity and positioning for Mexico, one of the world's 10 most popular tourist destinations. The brand needed to represent the best of Mexico from its millenary heritage, colonial legacy and diverse landscapes to its vibrant culture and modernity. Further complicating matters was the sheer breadth and variety of its considerable target audiences. Thus, any change made to the brand would need to add value to multiple marketing initiatives across a number of state, regional, and city tourism boards, as well as across varied travel industry sectors.

A multitier brand message and strategy was developed to appeal to key constituents, such as tourists, those working in the tourism industry, foreign investors, trade-makers, and international leaders. Effective relationships among all these stakeholders needed to be established, all while creating a powerful visual brand expression.

We thought the real challenge would be finding a singular focus within such a complex assignment, one that would allow us to take full advantage of Mexico's diverse history and culture. We then realized that the brand's focus should actually be the nation's richness and breadth; that bonds could be built through highlighting authentic cuisine, architectural grandeur, striking nature and compelling history. The new Mexico country brand would thus visualize a place that has been in evolution for centuries.

Color was used to demonstrate elements inherent to Mexico's culture, including merriment, history, optimism and cultural diversity, while each letter of the logo contained a decorative motif that represents a specific aspect of the offering as well as key features of the country.

New brand for Mexico

Advancing the development of the country brand was a global launch strategy. We designed a number of communication materials and initiatives, such as the Brand Ambassadorship Program, where leading personalities of the culture, art, trade, sports, and entertainment sectors were recruited to spread the new message beyond traditional media, reaching out worldwide to celebrate and promote a nation with a unique human spirit. Additionally, MBLM established a new digital platform that would delight visitors by enriching the content and creating a curated, personalized experience for each key market segment. Engaging planning tools were also created to leverage the nation's rich offerings. The site's colorful design furthered the essence of Mexico's country brand and reinforced the geographical and cultural diversity that makes Mexico a truly unique destination.

Mexico taught us that a rich, diverse country's brand should be celebrated, not contained, and that destinations, with their experiential nature, should demonstrate their essence at every turn. Our digital work in concert with the brand development expanded the ability of the brand to build closer connections with travelers. Aligning multiple constituents under a single country banner also demonstrated the importance of coordinated marketing initiatives that together could change perception, versus disparate efforts that siloed mindshare. As Eduardo Calderon, one of the founding partners of MBLM noted, "We were able to help shape a brand that different regions, cities and agencies could rally around and be proud of. It created a stronger Mexico country brand and clearly a more cohesive experience."

CULTURE AND ALIGNMENT

PAYPAL

Great brands are reflective of aligned and strong cultures, and the single biggest variable of any brand-building effort is employee adoption. Often overlooked or underappreciated, the time and energy required to effectively align and inspire internal stakeholders to evangelize on behalf of the brand is vital. Likewise, the role that all related partners, agencies, and vendors can play in building a brand is too frequently underutilized.

For nearly two decades, we've paid special attention to this aspect of brand launch and management, and have developed proprietary tools and techniques in order to effectively control the way a brand is evolved and nurtured. What began as software to manage the dissemination of assets and information for a brand in the mid-90's has evolved to become a platform for social collaboration, engagement, and real-time help. Our proprietary software solution, BrandOS, has developed into a simpler and smarter way to equip brands to grow, adapt, and deliver in a 24/7 dynamic global marketplace.

PayPal's Brand Central

One company using our software platform is PayPal. We were introduced to PayPal after they had rebranded. They were looking to sunset a range of different platforms and tools to simplify their brand management functions and promote internal adoption. PayPal needed to find ways to better arm their employees and partners with research and insights, and were also eager to inform and inspire internal teams and their networks of partners and agencies about their new brand. BrandOS provided them with a customized solution that effectively enabled their brand to be managed, maintained, and advanced across borders, geographies, and languages. From tactical requests to in-depth governance requirements, the software works to align cultures and brands by providing a platform for employees and partners to connect and bond with their brand, along with the resources to manage the brand more effectively.

PayPal taught us the importance not only of the message, but the medium. A powerful, user friendly tool that builds collaboration is a far more effective way of ensuring a marketing department's success than uncooperative systems and uninspired platforms.

1-2

PARADIGM SHIFT

The combination of a dramatically altered corporate dynamic and a seismic shift in the marketplace has prompted us to examine these forces in more detail. We have summarized three undeniable factors that are driving the need for a new paradigm in how we measure, build and manage brands.

BRANDS TODAY

The way we build, disseminate and engage with brands has changed drastically. The rules of the past—the one-way push approach from product to user and the role of a catchy name, logo or tagline—defines only part of the challenge for marketers today.

Brand is at the heart of this book. We have been in awe of the power of brands for over 20 years and are proud to have built some truly iconic ones. We have experienced their magic, been seduced by their siren song, and become devotees as well as architects of them.

We are also big believers in the *power* of brands. When a brand is strong, it commands price premiums, obtains a larger percentage of share, and out-performs its competitors. Brands also foster deep relationships and powerful bonds that can last a lifetime or more, passed down to the next generation. How many of us use the same laundry detergent our mothers did? Or still buy the same food brands?

That said, we'll be the first to admit that the ways we interacted with brands 20 years ago are no longer relevant for today. So, we wonder, why should our methods for measuring, building and managing brands remain the same? We believe the best brands remain optimized for the world we now live in. While change is unsettling, it's nevertheless clear that new thinking is needed to better align brands to the way they can thrive today. Brand is no longer just art and science; it's psychology, technology, and just a bit of new religion.

While the definition of a "brand" originally meant a mark made by burning, intended to indicate a specific kind or make (such as branding cattle), its context has largely remained the same: *a specific product, service or company; a relationship; a preferred connection; the sum of all associations, expectations and experiences that result in someone selecting a product or service over another*. We believe "brand" is a term that has been hijacked and co-opted in modern parlance. Diluted, overused, and too often relegated to the land of aesthetics or inane campaigns—places of meaningless superficiality and transience. As the real meaning of brand is being eroded, so too is its potential to be effectively leveraged by business.

Part of this is because just what is considered a brand and what a brand means has changed drastically. Traditionally, brands were products or com-panies seeking to define (or redefine) their reputation and deliver a service or function. Today, brands are apps, people, political parties, countries, and sports teams, to name only a few variants. The methods of the past—the push approach which literally broadcasts the brand's message to the masses in a one-way mode—are today only marginally relevant.

Let's take a step back. In the past, smart companies would use market research to segment consumers and define a target audience. They would quantify the perceptions, wants, and needs of this target audience, and then craft a brand positioning that leveraged the brand's strengths, differentiated the brand from the competition, and created a relevant and appealing proposition for target consumers. This brand strategy would be handed off to execute or activate with marketing, advertising and PR agencies, to name a few. Each would figure out the most effective ways to communicate the brand's key messages to reach and win over the target audience. A unique and memorable brand identity would be created, campaigns would be built, media relations would manage perceptions, reputation, and manage crisis. Brand managers would then maintain and adapt the brand to evolving needs.

This approach (in one form or another) has been industry best practice, at least in most Western industrialized countries, from the end of World War II until the Internet boom in the latter days of the twentieth century. And it's a very clear, linear chain, from establishing the value of a product or service to communicating it and finally optimizing it. Authorship of the brand is clear and the target consumer is fixed, defined and quantified.

If you're a brand today, just being noticed—rising above the saturation in the marketplace—is a major challenge. The average consumer now receives 5,000 marketing messages a day.[1] The average person now watches 12 hours of media each day and checks their phone over 110 times a day.[2] Staying relevant and remaining trusted is a perpetual struggle.

And this is because brands are being redefined by their *users*, not their creators. What a brand stands for—how it behaves, relates, and appears in a customer's life—is now heavily influenced by consumers. Perhaps that's why 84 percent of millennials don't trust traditional advertising.[3] Therefore, how you create a brand, how it communicates and interfaces (and how often) must evolve in order to be effective. Five out of six millennials connect with companies on social media, and are seven times more likely to give out their personal information to a trusted brand.[4]

Digital technology enables today's consumers to narrowly define what value means to them. They seek out sources and are influenced in a myriad of ways. And the source they most trust *is* each other (and their reliance on other consumers is increasing). According to Nielsen's 2015 Global Trust in Advertising Report, people don't trust advertising—at least not as much as they trust recommendations from friends and consumer opinions expressed online. The report, which surveyed more than 30,000 Internet respondents in 60 countries, shows that 84 percent of consumers say they trust "recommendations from people I know" above all other forms of advertising—and that by 20 percentage points. "Consumer opinions posted online" rank as the third most trusted source, at 66 percent.[5] We've all become very particular about what we consume and who we trust to inform us. The power of social media has created a strong influence network, where we'll trust a friend before we'll trust an advertisement or brand that's talking to us directly. That's another significant change if you're in the business of communicating a brand's value or essence.

Here's the thing that's becoming evident: In today's hyper-connected world, a traditional marketing approach is no longer relevant. Does anyone really believe that consumers these days are passively watching television commercials and then driven to try or prefer a brand? Today, companies need to both spread their message across numerous channels and platforms and be prepared to have their brand build a community of engagement.

How a brand interfaces, influences, and stays relevant nowadays requires an altogether new approach and a different makeup. We've uncovered a winning formula that presents an enormous opportunity for brands and those who market them. And it all begins with a new paradigm that builds, sustains, and measures ultimate brand relationships built on emotion.

Why does emotion matter for brands? According to a recent Gallup poll, a majority of consumers can't identify with leading brands.[6] The good news is that the opportunity for brands is immense—*if* they can find a way to bridge the gap. On a lifetime value basis, emotionally connected customers are more than twice as valuable as highly satisfied customers. Emotionally connected customers buy more of the brand's products and services, exhibit less price sensitivity, pay more attention to brand communications, and recommend the brand more frequently.[7]

Gallup also found that customers who are fully engaged represent an average 23 percent premium in terms of share of wallet, profitability, revenue, and relationship growth over the average customer. The same study showed that companies that engage both their employees and their customers gain a 240 percent boost in performance-related business outcomes.[8] Further, it has been found that an emotional response to an advertisement has far greater influence on a consumer's reported intent to buy a product than does the ad's content—by a factor of 3-to-1 for television ads and 2-to-1 for print ads.[9]

Navigating today's marketplace is made more difficult by brands proliferating (recall our earlier comment about misappropriation of the term "brand"), making it harder than ever to create distinctness and differentiation. Competitors copy faster than ever—everything from product features to messaging—resulting in a commodification of categories and the brands in them. Success today is predicated on building brands in omni-channel environments that draw consumers in and foster a community of influence and reciprocity. Brands must now remain two-way, agile and sensitive to market shifts, consumer behaviors and technological advancements.

TECHNOLOGY TOMORROW

In our interconnected and increasingly globalized lives, brand expectations have become elevated, demanding and immediate. One prime example is the supercomputers we carry inside our pockets and purses that have access to an entire ecosystem of enhancement. This one device, the ubiquitous smartphone, creates a profoundly personalized interface to a world of information, entertainment, work, family, and friends. The technology interface we enjoy changes what, how and when we consume brands. It alters how we share, how we learn and how we influence each other, too. The very meaning of what we know and what we believe is largely cast through the interface of technology. It can't be overstated how much technology has transformed our lives.

By 2020, the projected 9 billion connected mobile devices will exceed the global population by 16 percent.[10] Sensors and actuators in physical objects linked through wired and wireless networks (the Internet of Things) grew 300 percent in the last five years, and are expected to make a $2.7 to $6.2 trillion impact on the economy by 2025.[11]

In just a decade, digital, mobile, and social advancements have dramatically altered how we behave and react—and that includes how we interact with the brands in our lives. Through the proliferation of digital devices, mobility, cloud computing, social media and the Internet, technology, as we mentioned, is providing people with unprecedented access to information, the means to distribute it and the ability to connect with, learn from, and influence each other. Ultimately, technology is transforming the way people relate to each other and to the companies whose products and services they research, purchase, and discuss.

Technology is also creating new and more multifaceted ways to track and measure brands. Big data promises to answer tactical questions, including, "Who buys what? When? At what price?" "How can we link what consumers view, read, and hear to what they buy?" "What's most effective at attracting them?" These answers can result in short-term gains, in terms of increasing the next transaction, but big data can also try to contribute to more long-term concerns—strategic questions about customer retention, stickiness, and rela-tionships. Answering not just what will trigger the next purchase, but what will be the customer's life-time value and what can prevent them from leaving when offered a better competitive price, will be invaluable as brands and marketing research try to maintain a foothold in this new world. That said, big data can be overwhelming and it can be a challenge to read the signal from all the noise. For many, the continuously mounting data is as paralyzing as it is motivating, especially when faced with the challenge to sift, aggregate, prioritize or act based on these insights.

As technology has become increasingly pervasive, it has also become increasingly apparent that its impact is two-sided. In other words, there are consequences of technological advancement that people find beneficial and consequences they find detrimental. Technology creates a faster-moving, highly variable landscape, one that can both strengthen and threaten the bonds that strong brands depend on to survive. In the near future, the convergence of cloud computing, wearable mobile devices and ubiquitous interlinked sensors promises a paradigm shift as great as any that has taken place previously. In this new environment, where an individual's very senses will be augmented, brands will have a previously unimagined ability to engage people. However, this ability will in turn be counterbalanced by an unprecedented degree of responsibility to prevent information overload and to protect privacy.

To succeed in this newly redefined space, being intimate with brands—that is, the premise of this book—will need to become a critical consideration for businesses. If brands are to be welcome participants in an individual's perceptual net (or personal space) they will need to understand exactly how to cultivate not just a bond with their consumers, but an "intimate" relationship. The more personal or personalized the access a technology has to a person, the more heightened are the permissions and expectations on that brand.

A basic example of the new interplay between people and technology that many consumers have already experienced is haptic feedback. These are the sensors in our smartphones, smartwatches or "force feedback" joysticks in video game controllers[12] which provide a physical "feel" in response to actions driven by software and hardware. These haptic moments are creating a whole new computer/human interface.

Sensors are also behind the rapidly growing Internet of Things (IoT), linking networks to everyday objects, appliances and fixtures. The business implications are transforming the supply chain, providing just-in-time data around inventory. Machines send alerts for supplies or repairs and measure every aspect of their own performance. While many consumers may be unaware of the degree of impact the IoT has on their lives, their home networks today are becoming increasingly populated by devices like smart light fixtures, thermostats, smoke detectors, security systems, appliances and wearable devices that are all communicating through one network. Many would likely underestimate and be surprised by how many IPs (internet protocols or addresses which represent the different devices on their networks) there are today.

Less obvious though still burgeoning are sensor-driven technologies and applications—from self-replenishing supply chains and automated city man-agement systems to self-driving cars—that have analysts and many companies excited about the business opportunities. More recently, academics at the MIT Media Lab have been looking at a different side of the IoT, exploring how the ways we see, hear, think, and live will change when individuals can connect to it directly. They argue that, "[T]he modern world is filled with network-con-nected electronic sensors, but most of the data they produce are invisible to us, 'siloed' for use by specific applications. If we eliminate those silos and enable sensor data to be used by any network-connected device, the era of ubiqui-tous computing will truly arrive."[13] Specific to this topic, the MIT Media Lab is investigating questions such as: "Where do human senses begin and end when a person is linked to a sensor network that extends virtually everywhere and grafts information onto human perception?"[14] "What will 'presence' mean when people can funnel their perceptions freely across time, space and scale?"[15] They believe the new world of ubiquitous computing will be created by "context aggregators," tech companies that assemble sensor data into a new generation of applications.[16]

The forthcoming world of ubiquitous computing, context aggregation, and augmented perception presents both tremendous opportunities and chal-lenges for marketers. At the dawn of the Internet age, psychologist Mihaly Csikszentmihalyi wrote about the potential of the Internet as a medium for staging experience. He focused on the possibility of creating Web experiences that would elicit "a state of intense emotional involvement and timelessness that comes from immersive and challenging activities".[17] And while the Internet has generally fallen short of delivering truly immersive experiences, it seems that with ubiquitous computing this promise may finally be realizable.

This appears to be what is driving numerous technology companies in their investments in virtual and augmented reality. Google Glass was an early example of a wearable technology, which offered new ways to access information, share content, and interact with the environment.[18] Google also introduced Universal Analytics, which can integrate offline and online metrics, a capability that will only become more relevant in a sensor-enabled world. Compare this to the Apple Watch. The Apple Watch is more than the company's first foray into wearable devices; it is Apple's "most personal device yet," enabling people to connect with each other and with information in new ways, physically touching them for alerts, notifications, and health monitoring. In effect, the device extends the wearer's senses.[19]

Facebook may be the company that has most tipped its hand with its vision of how ubiquitous sensor-enabled computing can transform the consumer experience. Regarding the company's recent acquisition of Oculus VR, Mark Zuckerberg posted: "After games, we're going to make Oculus a platform for many other experiences. Imagine enjoying a courtside seat at a game, studying in a classroom of students and teachers all over the world, or consulting with a doctor face to face—just by putting on goggles in your home. This is really a new communication platform. By feeling truly present, you can share unbounded spaces and experiences with the people in your life. Imagine sharing not just moments with your friends online, but entire experiences and adventures."[20]

What Zuckerberg is talking about (and what Google and Apple seem to be alluding to) is a shift in what technology *is*. Technology has typically been thought of as an enabler, a tool to connect us with information and other people and to provide us with computational power beyond our individual capabilities. With ubiquitous computing, technology transcends enablement to become the very environment in which we perceive the world, interact with others, entertain ourselves, and get things done.

However, as the emerging environment of Internet-worked sensors reshape the consumer experience, key issues must also be addressed. First among these are concerns about privacy and security, not to mention means of processing the unfathomable ocean of information that all these connected devices are creating. Connected individuals will need to be able to exert some control to protect their privacy and security (by limiting or preventing access from snoopers and hackers) as well as their sanity (by limiting the flow of information they experience). Brands will need to tread cautiously between enablement and overreaching.

From a marketing perspective, the environment of connected and sensor-enhanced consumers creates exciting new possibilities—which bring with them their own challenges. When technology becomes the environment itself, brands become able to personalize, be more context-relevant and predictive in an individual's life. In this new world which is both exciting and scary, individuals will be able to exert even more control over which brands they interact with and the degree of interaction they allow. The very same is true for brands themselves— more control and higher potential for intimate interactions. What emerges has new rules, with brand relationships becoming far more bidirectional.

The new paradigm of Brand Intimacy, we believe, is an essential framework for brands that need to navigate the new complexities of technological realities.

Why? Understanding the intricacies and mechanisms of brand intimacy will help businesses better focus their resources to carve out a meaningful place in the perceptual/experiential networks individuals maintain. This framework will also help companies avoid and/or respond to relationship pitfalls that might otherwise lead to consumer indifference. In effect, our approach is the currency of the forthcoming consciousness and experience-expanding world in which consumers and brands are brokering information flow, privacy, security, and identity. Ultimately, understanding how to leverage technology will bring with it the power to build better brand bonds—bonds that can endure and are mutually beneficial.

BRAINS NOW: HOW EMOTION DRIVES CHOICES AND DECISIONS

We now know more about how the human brain processes information and triggers our behaviors than ever before. Even with all the technological advancements and resulting brand transformation, it may be the discoveries in neuroscience that have the largest impact about how we think about brands today. We now know that up to 90 percent of the decisions we make are based on emotion.[21] Take a minute and read that again; *almost every decision we make* is based on emotion, not rational thought and measured consideration. Our decisions are the result of less deliberate, linear, and controlled processes than we would like to believe. This is true whether it is a personal decision, a professional one, or even a group decision.[22]

Yet for over 1,000 years in the West, philosophers, scientists, and even psychologists did not focus their attention on human emotion. The general opinion was that emotions were a base part of humanity, a vestige of our "animal" past, and that rationality was what separated Homo sapiens from other, lesser animals.

This attitude began to change somewhat in the twentieth century, with considerable focus being brought on the psychological and psychiatric treatment of neuroses and psychoses. But the subject of what emotions are and what their evolutionary or survival value is to human beings was not addressed to any great extent until the last 20 years.

A big change in the field was sparked by the discoveries of neurophysiologist Antonio Damasio, reported in his 1999 book, *The Feeling of What Happens*. In it, Damasio reports: "Work from my laboratory has shown that emotion is integral to the process of reasoning and decision making, for worse and for better. This may sound a bit counterintuitive, at first, but there is evidence to support it. The finding comes from the study of several individuals who were entirely rational in the way they ran their lives up to the time when, as a result of neurological damage in specific sites of their brains, they lost a certain class of emotions and, in a momentous parallel development, lost their ability to make rational decisions...These findings suggest that selective reduction of emotion is at least as prejudicial for rationality as excessive emotion. It certainly does not seem true that reason stands to gain from operating without the leverage of emotion. On the contrary, emotion probably assists reasoning, especially when it comes to personal and social matters involving risk and conflict. I suggested that certain levels of emotion processing probably point us to the sector of the decision-making space where our reason can operate most efficiently. I did not suggest, however, that emotions are a substitute for reason or that emotions decide for us. It is obvious that emotional upheavals can lead to irrational decisions. The neurological evidence simply suggests that selective absence of emotion is a problem. Well–targeted and well–deployed emotion seems to be a support system without which the edifice of reason cannot operate properly."[23]

If Damasio's work was the catalyst, then the Nobel Prize-winning work by psychologist Daniel Kahneman was the revolution that changed our way of thinking *about* thinking. Through dozens of experiments over decades, Kahneman created a new model to explain how people think and make decisions. Kahneman created a construct, called System 1 and System 2, to replace left and right brain, respectively. System 1 handles basic tasks and calculations like walking, breathing, and determining the value of 1 + 1; System 2 takes on more complicated, abstract decision making and calculations, like 435 x 23. System 1 is more driven by intuition, snap judgments, and emotion. System 2 is driven more by reason. Kahneman explains the differences as follows: "'System 1 does X' is a shortcut for 'X occurs automatically.' And 'System 2 is mobilized to do Y' is a shortcut for 'arousal increases, pupils dilate, attention is focused, and activity Y is performed.'"[24]

What may be most important about Kahneman's work is his finding that most human decisions are made emotionally, and that the function of human reason is to justify those decisions after the fact.

"The implication is clear: as the psychologist Jonathan Haidt said in another context 'The emotional tail wags the rational dog'…Until now I have mostly described it [System 2] as a more or less acquiescent monitor, which allows considerable leeway to System 1. I have also presented System 2 as active in deliberate memory search, complex computations, comparisons, planning, and choice. Self-criticism is one of the functions of System 2. In the context of attitudes, however, System 2 is more of an apologist for the emotions of System 1 than a critic of those emotions—an endorser rather than an enforcer. Its search for information and arguments is mostly constrained to information that is consistent with existing beliefs, not with an intention to examine them. An active, coherence-seeking System 1 suggests solutions to an undemanding System 2."[25]

The idea of humans as rational actors who make decisions to buy or use products and services in purely rational thinking is clearly flawed. We've seen firsthand that brands that do well today are the ones that touch peoples' emotions in deep, meaningful, and authentic ways. Features, specifications can be noise—additional and largely unneeded fodder for System 2 to rationalize emotion-based decisions after they are already made.

Jonathan Haidt, in his book *The Righteous Mind: Why Good People Are Divided by Politics and Religion,* notes, "The mind is divided, like a rider on an elephant, and the rider's job is to serve the elephant. The rider is our conscious reasoning—the stream of words and images of which we are fully aware. The elephant is the other 99 percent of mental processes—the ones that occur outside of awareness but that actually govern most of our behavior."[26]

What this suggests is that, in order to impact and affect decision making, you have to appeal and connect to people's emotions. Although perhaps counterintuitive to prevailing sentiment, playing to rational considerations is not a compelling motivator; in fact, it *limits* the potential of building bonds. The bottom line is that scientific and academic data has proven that human beings react intuitively to everything they perceive and base their responses on those reactions rather quickly. Within the first second of seeing something, hearing something, or meeting another person, impressions are made and actions are born. *Intuitions come first.*[27] This suggests that traditional models, constructs, and methodologies that we have used for decades to drive our marketing and communications efforts outweigh the importance of rational thinking, rendering them outdated and faulty.

One particular aspect of the work done by Kahneman and his peers has been widely adopted by Behavioral Science and Behavioral Economics. Behavioral Economics aims to change the way economists think about the way humans perceive value and express preferences. This line of thinking, which uses psychological experimentation to develop theories about decision making, has identified a range of biases related to people's perceptions of value and expressed preferences. In short, people don't make considered choices; they are not always benefits-maximizing, cost-minimizing, and self-interested. They go with what feels right, with what *feels* like the right option. They are influenced by readily available information, and that includes our memories and salient information in the environment. We tend to live in the moment, resist change, are poor predictors of future behavior, are subject to distorted memory and are impacted by psychological and emotional states.[28] Our thinking is subject to insufficient knowledge, feedback, and processing capacity, as well as cognitive biases and emotions. This makes the context of our decision making extremely influential. Additionally, behavioral scientists have recognized that humans do not make choices in isolation. We are social beings with social preferences, trust and reciprocity play a key role.[29]

Behavioral Science also suggests that we use "stories" as a way help us organize the information we receive, help us remember it, and help us make sense of the world. Since our brains have a limited amount of processing power and memory, shortcuts like stories and heuristics help us to make sense of our environment. This starts first thing in the morning as we consume information and interact with the world around us continuing through the day and into our dreams. This can become an important opportunity for marketers—using stories to impact how we notice, connect, and consider brands. Combining the significant role emotion can play with the power of a strong narrative establishes a new fundamental for effective brand building.

1-3

APPROACHES
AND MODELS

Facing these market forces as brand builders, we witnessed clients paralyzed by the marketing approaches and methodologies currently in use. Few leverage emotion, or are based on a real understanding of the way people actually make decisions. Still, in exploring them we gained a better understanding of their shortcomings in measuring and facilitating the bonds we form with brands.

HIERARCHICAL DECISION MODEL

The hierarchical decision model (HDM) is a logical behavioral model that tracks what is assumed to be the natural progression that people go through when experiencing a brand, typically through detailing rational marketing measures. It generally starts with awareness and advances to the highest stage (usually loyalty or advocacy).

HIERARCHICAL DECISION MODEL

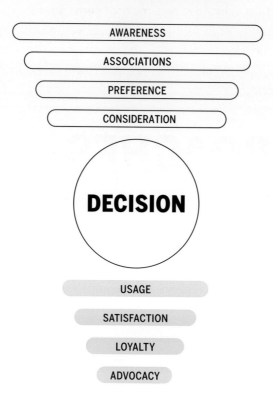

AWARENESS

ASSOCIATIONS

PREFERENCE

CONSIDERATION

DECISION

USAGE

SATISFACTION

LOYALTY

ADVOCACY

This type of model alternatively divides between pre-purchase and purchase, sometimes also called the Loyalty Ladder. It is often used to measure a brand's maturity and help determine where it needs to improve. The theory is that if you understand where stakeholders are along these measures, you can develop strategies and messaging that persuade them to advance to a higher level. This model assumes only a downward trajectory (moving from awareness to consideration to beyond) and measures where consumers are on a spectrum of decision. The various components utilized are based on consumer purchase decisions, post-purchase behavior and attempts to isolate when and how brands move higher in terms of needs. The model also assumes (incorrectly) that there is a definitive link between purchase intention and action, which has been shown to have little or no correlation with actual behavior.

This approach generally does not determine why a brand may be in a certain position, or if indeed these "decision-making" steps are indicative of the natural way people make decisions. In fact, what we know today suggests this does not reflect a consumer's reality. The hierarchical decision model creates artificial layers of nuance, when in fact decision making is instinctive, fast, and based on emotion. The HDM does give us a clear roadmap for assessing other models and approaches. We moved to exploring more of the post-decision territories that focus on the satisfaction and loyalty areas.

SATISFACTION AND THE NET PROMOTER SCORE

Net promoter scores (NPS) are a popular technique with many Fortune 1000 companies used to measure the loyalty between a company and its customers. The net promoter score is calculated based on responses to a single question: *How likely is it that you would recommend our company/product/service to a friend or colleague?* The scoring for this answer is most often based on a 0 to 10 scale.[30] The relative simplicity of the methodology and its corresponding NPS score gives researchers and executives a straightforward and easy to understand tool to gain a reading on the relative performance of the brand.

Developed by (and a registered trademark of) Fred Reichheld, Bain & Company, and Satmetrix Systems, the NPS score was introduced by Reichheld in his 2003 *Harvard Business Review* article, "One Number You Need to Grow"[31]. NPS can be as low as –100 (where everybody is a detractor) or as high as +100 (everybody is a promoter). An NPS that is positive (i.e., higher than zero) is felt to be good, and an NPS of +50 is considered excellent.[32]

We have seen the impact of NPS firsthand in executive offices around the globe. But while it has gained popularity among business leaders, it has also attracted controversy from academic and market research circles. Since it lacks a predictive quality (dealing more with the here and now versus the future) and has a singular focus around the intention to recommend, this model can be limiting for measuring the more complex nature of the bonds we form with brands today.

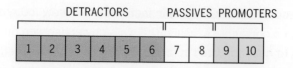

SATISFACTION

DETRACTORS   PASSIVES PROMOTERS

| 1 | 2 | 3 | 4 | 5 | 6 | 7 | 8 | 9 | 10 |

NPS = DETRACTORS - PROMOTERS

LOYALTY

Loyalty has long been considered the ultimate goal of one's desired customer base, and most companies want to increase their percentage of these valued users. Traditionally, brand loyalty refers to a consumer's preference to buy a particular brand in a product category. It occurs because consumers perceive that the brand offers the right product features, images, or level of quality at the right price. This perception becomes the foundation for a new buying habit.

At one end of the spectrum, repeat purchase is often used as a standard for loyalty. At the other end, companies like Walker—a leading loyalty research and consulting firm—use a range of attitudinal (e.g., customers like working with a company and have a positive attitude toward the company) and behavioral (e.g., customers' intention to continue doing business with a company, or recommend the company to others) metrics to measure loyalty and the stability of a company's customer base.[33]

Loyalty is valued for several key reasons:

- **Higher sales volume:** The average United States company loses half of its customers every five years, equating to a 13 percent annual loss of customers. This highlights the challenges of trying to grow a customer base. Achieving even 1 percent annual growth requires increasing sales to customers, both existing and new, by 14 percent. It's clear that limiting customer loss and increasing retention is extremely valuable.

- **Premium pricing ability:** Studies have shown that as brand loyalty increases, consumers are less sensitive to price changes. Generally, they are willing to pay more for their preferred brand because they perceive some unique value in the brand that other alternatives do not provide.

- **Retain, rather than seek:** Brand loyalists are willing to seek and search for their favorite brand and are less sensitive to competitive promotions. The result can be lower costs for advertising, marketing, and distribution.[34]

However, the use of loyalty as an ultimate measure has been effectively challenged by The Ehrenberg-Bass Institute, who have shown empirically that loyalty to one brand is generally only practiced by those who are very low users of a category, and therefore is not something a brand need aspire to. Indeed, 100 percent-loyal buyers are not especially important to one's sales; they are few in number and are not particularly heavy buyers of the brand or product to begin with.[35] The majority of consumers tend to have ongoing relationships with several brands, with one usually consumed or purchased more often than the others.[36]

Byron Sharp, in his book, *How Brands Grow,* echoes this thinking. He debunks that oft-repeated fact that 20 percent of your customers represent 80 percent of your sales. After reviewing multiple categories, he found that the number never got higher than 50 percent of customers representing 20 percent of business.[37] Sharp goes on to suggest that loyalty metrics do not reflect the marketing strategy or image of the brand. In fact, he argues that customer loyalty is largely a myth; customers are at best "promiscuous loyals," flitting fickly between alternate rival brands based on availability (e.g., 72 percent of Coke drinkers also buy Pepsi (UK)[38]).

It is clear there is still debate surrounding the idea of loyalty, but whether you believe it has value (or sufficient value) or not, loyalty can be an outcome of brand intimacy. Consumers who form close personal bonds with a brand are more likely to want that brand, rather than its competitors. They are also likely to be the brand's most fervent advocates.

Where loyalty and brand intimacy differ is that, in essence, loyalty looks at behaviors and/or attitudes—not what underpins them. Loyalty is not necessarily driven by brand; loyalty can also result from responsive service or customized products. Brand intimacy, on the other hand, focuses on human-brand relationships and their psychological drivers.

WALKER'S LOYALTY MATRIX

The Walker model examines attitudes and behaviors and forms a thesis for how people become loyal to different brands (notably B2B) and what loyalty means. Walker found that conventional metrics of customer affinity—namely satisfaction, repurchase intent, and recommendations—were, in isolation, insufficient metrics to fully understand the complexities of customer behavior and its underlying motivating forces. They developed four "loyalty quadrants" based on attitude and behavior, as a way to segment levels of loyalty.

They are:

1. **Truly loyal**: Refers to customers who enjoy working with a company, have positive associations about them, and plan to continue to do so. They are also more likely to increase spending with the company and recommend it to others.
2. **Accessible**: A mixed bag group, one that does not plan to continue working with the company in question; however, they will still speak well of them. This group often makes up a small percentage of a company's customers and consists of customers who no longer need the company's products or services.
3. **Trapped**: These are customers that continue to do business with the company, but are not happy about doing so. They are often trapped by contracts, a lack of a substitute, or barriers to switching companies. They are unlikely to increase business with the company and are more likely to find other options.

4. **High risk**: These are customers who do not intend to return or continue doing business with the company and do not hold it in high regard. They will talk poorly about the company and will likely not be a customer for long.

These four groups are plotted as quadrants on a Loyalty Matrix, with attitude as the vertical axis and behavior as the horizontal axis. This matrix is used as a framework for measuring loyalty and is meant to help better understand business strategies in a practical way.

This is a valuable tool and provides a view into customer stability and a break-down of customer loyalty. While it *does* measure some emotional components in defining its segments, it does not use emotion as a *foundation*. Further, loyalty itself, as a value measure, has been questioned (which raises a separate issue about the best way to measure customer retention).

WALKER'S LOYALTY MATRIX

	ACCESSIBLE	**TRULY LOYAL**
ATTITUDE		
	HIGH RISK	TRAPPED

BEHAVIOR

Next is a series of models that explore the intrinsic value in brands, treating them more as an asset than a relationship.

YOUNG & RUBICAM BRAND ASSET VALUATOR (BAV) MODEL

The BAV Model, developed by global advertising agency Young & Rubicam, measures brand value by leveraging four key considerations. These include:

- **Differentiation**: the ability of a brand to be distinct from its competitive set;
- **Relevance**: the actual and perceived importance of the brand to its target audience;
- **Esteem**: the perceived quality of the brand and consumer perceptions about the increasing or declining popularity of the brand; and
- **Knowledge**: the extent of consumer awareness of a brand and their understanding of its identity.

According to the model, the process of a brand's growth typically follows the order of Differentiation, Relevance, Esteem, and finally, Knowledge. Together, differentiation and relevance determine brand strength, which can be an indicator of the brand's future performance. Esteem and knowledge together combine to determine brand stature, which is a measure of the *current* performance of the brand and represents its status among consumers.

On a grid that Young & Rubicam calls the Power Grid, brands can be plotted to compare their performance, with brand strength as the vertical axis and brand stature as the horizontal axis. As a brand grows, it begins by increasing its brand strength, followed by an increase in its brand stature.[39]

This model provides valuable insight into understanding the strengths and weaknesses of a brand. But it is observational in nature and one-sided in scope, meaning it looks at what consumers do and how they think, without considering how a brand's interactions can contribute to measuring these values. The four measures are also very rational-centered and don't take into account emotion as a driving force behind behavior.

INTERBRAND VALUATION MODEL

In examining alternate methodologies that approached our way of thinking on brand intimacy, we also looked at the Interbrand Valuation model, which provides information on how to deploy a brand in order to create brand equity. With the advent of valuation in the 1980s, Interbrand pioneered an approach that examined how a brand contributes to business performance and provided a series of activities and recommendations to help ensure continued improvement.

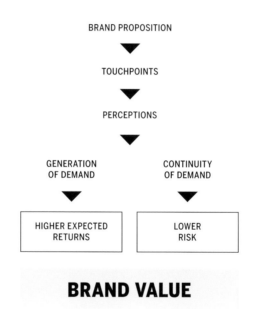

INTERBRAND'S BRAND VALUATION MODEL

BRAND PROPOSITION

TOUCHPOINTS

PERCEPTIONS

GENERATION OF DEMAND   CONTINUITY OF DEMAND

HIGHER EXPECTED RETURNS   LOWER RISK

BRAND VALUE

Interbrand's model considers three key levers:

1. The brand's financial performance; i.e., the economic profits generated by the products and services.
2. The role of brand, which measures the portion of the decision to purchase that is attributable to the brand relative to other forces (e.g., price, design, features). This portion is then expressed as a percentage, known as the Role of Brand Index (RBI).
3. Last, brand strength, which is a diagnostic tool for measuring brand performance relative to competition. It measures the brand's ability to create loyalty, and identifies the brand's strengths and weaknesses.[40]

Analyses of these three levers were combined to create one single measure of the brand's contribution to its organization's business results—its Brand Value. This metric has since been used as a strategic tool to evaluate, inform, and guide aspects of the business. This metric is used both for one-off business cases and for ongoing brand management applications.

We found that, while this approach *can* provide rich data and important recommendations to help a brand improve business performance, the levers are all very rational-centered and do not seem to consider the role of emotion. It is also extremely focused on mapping symptoms as opposed to diagnosing problems.

To contrast with the more financially-minded brand asset models, we wanted to also acknowledge the many intriguing and relevant methods for measuring the emotional aspects of brands that exist today.

CUSTOMER INTIMACY

Customer intimacy is a broad term, rather than a specific process. It focuses on the individual; specifically, it refers to the discipline or business approach that brings an organization closer to its customers by focusing on an understanding of their wants and needs, to better enable individualized product, service, or communications delivery. "Companies that excel in customer intimacy combine detailed customer knowledge with operational flexibility so they can respond quickly to almost any need, from customizing a product to fulfilling special requests."[41] Mutual understanding, value perception, and closeness are all hallmarks of customer intimacy. Once value may have been defined by price; however, for many that concept has been expanded and now encompasses convenience of purchase, after-sale service, dependability, and so on.[42]

Customer intimacy also involves meeting the changing expectations of a brand's users. Businesses that pursue customer intimacy frequently tailor and adjust products and services to fit customer wants. This can be expensive, but customer-intimate companies believe it is worth the cost, as they seek to build customer loyalty for the long term. They typically look at the customer's lifetime value to the company, not the value of any single transaction.

Customer intimacy has been found to positively impact relationship commitment levels, behavioral loyalty/repurchase intentions, customer availability, advisor status, and customer-induced word of mouth. Yet for all its growth in popularity, the term itself has not been widely adopted.[43]

When a popular business book highlighted the importance of customer intimacy, they suggested it was one of three business models a company could choose, those being: (1) customer intimacy—delivering what specific customers want; (2) operations excellence—delivering quality, price, and ease of purchase and use; and (3) product leadership—creating the best products and services.[44] Today, several articles have suggested a company need not choose one but can combine these approaches.

Interestingly, it has been suggested that business managers should also embrace the "often forgotten value of non-rational relationship aspects… The value perception dimension of customer intimacy is not purely rational. Emotional motives, simply enjoying the relationship with the supplier, also matter."[45] Important to note: Where customer and brand intimacy differ is that customer intimacy does not *directly* address the bonds people form with brands; this is the sole domain of brand intimacy.

BRAND ENGAGEMENT

Brand engagement is a broad term/approach, used by many to mean different things. Generally speaking, it refers to promoting interaction between a customer and a brand, rather than just driving sales. Jay Henderson, director of strategy for IBM, wrote, "I think of engagement as representing two-way communication between a brand and consumers...Today, brands can listen more effectively to customers and, as a result, deliver a more informed and tailored marketing message. Moreover, there is a huge opportunity for marketers to extend the reach of their marketing campaigns by encouraging customers to share their purchases, their experiences, and their likes—making a good customer not just those who transact, but also those who share."[46]

Brand engagement happens through various forms of brand-consumer communications, which occur at different points of contact, or "touchpoints." These touchpoints include advertising, social media, retail environments, and the products/services themselves, and allow brands and consumers to interact and share with each other, and build a relationship. The goal of the brand here is to drive consumer loyalty and sentiment toward the brand, eventually increasing the consumer's value as a customer.

An interesting brand engagement study by Gensler in 2013 sought to discover the difference between a transaction versus a relationship. They wanted to explore the emotional connection between consumers and brands, and hypothesized that true engagement is emotional, not transactional. They surveyed 2,838 consumers in the United States and found that "high-emotion" customers were more satisfied, purchased their favorite brands more often, and were more likely to recommend the brand. "High-emotion" consumers are nearly two times more likely than "low-emotion" consumers to say that their favorite brand is a part of their daily routine. They also found people connected with brands that shared their values and delivered quality.[47]

Engagement suggests a two-way relationship, which is important; most other approaches in the field are one-way. However, success is generally seen as the number of shares or one's earned reach/influence. Brand engagement doesn't tell you how to create a brand people will bond with; it just indicates that engaging with them is an important component of brand building. Brands based on rational thought, for example, could try and engage with their audiences and still be unsuccessful because they are not adopting those principles which will help ensure their ability to build bonds. Because engagement involves customers acting and participating with a brand, it can be viewed as a contributor to brand intimacy.

But brand engagement is not intimacy and does not ensure intimacy. Brand intimacy requires time to allow a relationship to develop through the accumulation of relevant experience and knowledge, which is more than an engagement program can deliver by itself.

LOVEMARKS

On the surface, Lovemarks bears a resemblance to brand intimacy. Its website states, "Lovemarks reach your heart as well as your mind, creating an intimate, emotional connection that you just can't live without. Ever."[48] Developed by former Saatchi & Saatchi CEO Kevin Roberts and seen as the ultimate goal of a brand, to qualify as a Lovemark a brand must be nominated by a site visitor, who shares a story about the brand. There is also a 30-question Lovemark Profiler, which states, "If you can answer YES to all the questions, congratulations, your brand is a Lovemark!"[49] The questions target individual opinions about the brand; for example: "Are you confident that _____ would never do anything you wouldn't want to be associated with?" "Does _____ fit perfectly to the way you dream about yourself?"[50] Site visitors can then vote on whether they love a certain brand and whether they feel it should be added or removed from the list of the Top 200 Lovemarks. (For example, 3,665 people voted that they love Apple while 375 voted to lose it.[51]) Because Lovemarks are based on consumer opinions rather than more deep-seated motivations, they tend to be highly popular brands that have passionate fans, not just customers. This makes a Lovemark an admirable and valuable status for a brand to achieve.

However, while consumers who have an intimate relationship with a brand are also likely to be passionate fans, this is where the similarity between Lovemark status and brand intimacy ends. Lovemarks does not address what is the true focus of brand intimacy—the underlying psychology that describes why and how a close, personal relationship is formed, maintained, and lost between a consumer and a brand. Additionally, Lovemarks' idea of falling in love with a brand and buying only that brand is not reflective of actual consumer behavior; it's a popular exaggeration, as was explained in the Loyalty section of this chapter. Also, Lovemarks doesn't really address the causes and effects of "falling out of love" with a brand, which as we all know from personal relationships, happens relatively frequently.

Lovemarks serves as an outline of a particular marketing philosophy and assigns a status to those brands that most successfully embody that philosophy. Although these brands do receive a love score, these scores are based on consumer clicks on the Lovemarks website, making it more of a participation-based demonstration rather than a statistical representation of consumer sentiment. This also means that only the most zealous fans have an impact on the results, while brand intimacy accounts for and includes different levels of intimacy between brands and consumers.

In fact, in Kevin Roberts's book, *Lovemarks: The Future beyond Brands*, he answers the question, "What makes a truly great love stand out?" with, "Mystery, Sensuality, and Intimacy," suggesting that intimacy might just be one piece of the Lovemarks puzzle. Overall, Lovemarks is a theory supported mainly by anecdotal evidence, used to inspire rather than inform marketing strategy and conceptualize the success of the world's most beloved brands.

EMOTIONAL BRANDING

Emotional branding describes (and advocates for) a more emotional approach to marketing strategy, one reached by understanding consumers, engaging their senses, and creating more innovative brands. Written by co-founder and former CEO of Desgippes Gobé (now Brandimage) Marc Gobé, *Emotional*

Branding: The New Paradigm for Connecting Brands to People uses countless branding anecdotes and case studies to explain various elements of emotional branding. It offers a significant change in perspective compared to most marketing materials and extols the virtues of linking brands with emotion.

Gobé's *Emotional Branding* starts by looking at successful brands from recent history to glean valuable lessons in brand strategy, all of which relate to the overarching philosophy of emotional branding. The book begins by introducing the concept of emotional branding, explaining, "By emotional, I mean how a brand engages consumers on the level of the senses and emotions; how a brand comes to life for people and forges a deeper, lasting connection."[52] He goes on to explore how emotional branding relates to consumer demographics and trends, sensorial experiences, and brand innovation.

Like brand intimacy, *Emotional Branding* suggests that emotional connections build stronger, more effective brands. The two approaches appear conceptually compatible, even though they employ different techniques and serve different roles. *Emotional Branding* looks at branding history to inform our perspective, while *Brand Intimacy* analyzes the psychology of consumers to draw meaningful conclusions about their relationships with brands (and has proprietary data and research behind it).

Emotional Branding does little to address the different levels of brand-consumer bonds and how these bonds can change and weaken over time. Rather, the book focuses on ways to create and strengthen connections with consumers without capturing or explaining the stages in these relationships or the process by which consumers grow to bond with brands. For the most part, the book also does not explain or leverage modern understandings about how the brain works and how people make decisions. Although consumer attitudes as preferences are often described, little is done to explain the psychology behind the way consumers feel toward brands.

1-4

UNDERSTANDING INTIMACY

We wanted to learn more about human intimacy to test our hypothesis that people can form relationships with brands in the same way they form relationships with other people. This required a comprehensive understanding of the meaning of intimacy and how thinking on this topic has evolved and advanced over time.

THE DEFINITIONS OF INTIMACY

"Intimacy" has many connotations—perhaps the most widely known is the physical form of intimacy—but in virtually every case, intimacy refers to a relationship in which there is a feeling of closeness. There have been a variety of definitions of intimacy. Intimacy has been described as, "[K]nowing that I am not alone in the universe...the sharing of closeness, of bonding, of reciprocation. It is the engulfing of warmth and care. It is the experiencing of another."[53] Marketing academician Barbara Stern cites the following definition of intimacy: "A knowledge of the core of something, an understanding of the inmost parts, that which is indicative of one's deepest nature and marked by close physical, mental, and social association."[54] Psychologist Dan McAdams notes intimacy "refers to the sharing of one's innermost being, or essence."[55] He states that no other desire may be more compelling than the desire for intimacy and asserts that this "universal intimacy motive" is "fundamental" to human experience—though the degree of motivation varies by individual.

Indeed, intimate relationships play a central role in the overall human experience.[56] Aristotle, one of the first thinkers to address how humans form relationships, suggested that utility, pleasure, and virtue were the underlying factors for all relationships. Only those relationships built from virtue and based on partners liked for being themselves had the potential be long-lasting. This was the prevailing thinking on intimate relationships until the twentieth century,[57] when William James penned *The Principles of Psychology*. In it, he described the many ways in which the self can manifest, including the material self, the social self, the spiritual self, and the pure ego.[58] James felt a person's self-concept must be seen within the context of his/her relationships with other people. Freud would later examine relationships with this in mind, and proposed that a human being's first encounter with intimate behavior is with his or her mother, during the act of breast-feeding.[59] This thinking has been developed further in social psychology, as noted by Maren Cardillo: as a child matures, her or his need for autonomy and individuation influences his or her intimate interactions with peers. These interactions, often characterized by autonomy, sensitivity, empathetic concern, and the ability to verbalize emotions, have been found to influence the formation of intimate friendships later on.[60]

During adolescence, much changes, both in terms of social development and the role and focus of family and friends. This is the period when the amount of time a child spends with their parents is reduced by half.[61] Adolescents seek out those undergoing similar physical and emotional changes and prioritize increased interactions related to their new needs and stresses. Thus, intimate interactions increase between friends during this life stage because they provide teens with a foundation for self-understanding and clarification. Some also suggest intimate relationships in early life ultimately give rise to an individual's personality.[62]

As we mature, intimacy can take on additional nuances. Robert Sternberg, a psychologist and psychometrician, has developed a triangular theory of love which includes intimacy as one of its three components. In his theory, intimacy encompasses feelings of attachment, closeness, connectedness, and bondedness. It is the emotional part of the triangle (whereas the other two areas, passion and commitment, form the physical and cognitive components, respectively).[63]

While the predominant thinking in psychology has largely focused on the romantic aspects of intimacy (versus platonic, parental, or friendship relationships), Perlman and Fehr identify three consistent themes across multiple interpretations that are relevant and aligned to our discussion of intimacy as it relates to branding:

1. The closeness and interdependence of partners,
2. The extent of self-disclosure, and
3. The warmth or affection experienced.[64]

ERIKSON'S APPROACH TO INTIMACY

Psychologist Erik Erikson articulated what is generally accepted as the definitive definition of intimacy in his work on the stages of psychosocial development, which identifies eight stages through which a healthily developing human should pass as they go from infancy to late adulthood. In each stage, the person confronts, and hopefully masters, new challenges. Each stage builds upon the successful completion of earlier stages; likewise, the challenges of stages not successfully completed may be expected to reappear as problems in the future.[65]

Erikson found that intimacy is a stage that generally occurs in young adulthood, when people begin to share their true thoughts and feelings with non-family members in an exploration of relationships that can lead to longer-term commitment. Once people have established their identities, Erikson felt they are ready to make long-term commitments to others.[66] They become capable of forming intimate, reciprocal relationships (e.g., through close friendships or marriage) and willingly make the sacrifices and compromises that such relationships require. Avoiding intimacy, or fearing commitment and relationships, can lead to isolation, loneliness, and sometimes depression. He asserted that, "Intimacy is really the ability to fuse your identity with someone else's without the fear that you're going to lose something yourself."[67] This definition is significant, because it identifies the two elements that are essential to our understanding of intimacy as it can relate to building brand relationships:

1. First, the idea of fused identities describes a relationship in which there is a close personal connection and a feeling of belonging together.

2. Second, the thought regarding a lack of fear—a sense of security people develop in a relationship through experience and over time, which enables them to take down their emotional "walls" and be themselves.

MODELING INTIMACY

Intimate relationships can take a number of forms, but these two elements—a feeling of fused identities and a sense of security that enables people to feel that they can be themselves—are always present, whether they're consciously considered or not.

Decades after Erikson's seminal work, additional thinking, constructs and models have been developed to articulate the process of forming relationships. Interestingly, several models have already been established to measure or consider intimacy as related to advertising and marketing.

Levinger's Five-Stage Model: Psychologist George Levinger proposed a five-stage model related to the development of an adult romantic relationship, which has since been used and adapted to study other types of relationships, both personal and commercial. The model's five stages are: Acquaintance, Build-up, Continuation, Deterioration, and Ending[68].

Levinger developed this model to explain how and why heterosexual married couples come together and fall apart, and described the process as somewhat of an inevitability. However, the model is also used to study a variety of relationships, oftentimes serving as a road map for preventing or avoiding the Deterioration and Ending stages of the process.[69]

LEVINGER'S FIVE-STAGE MODEL

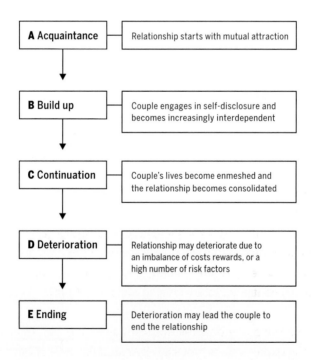

A Acquaintance — Relationship starts with mutual attraction

B Build up — Couple engages in self-disclosure and becomes increasingly interdependent

C Continuation — Couple's lives become enmeshed and the relationship becomes consolidated

D Deterioration — Relationship may deteriorate due to an imbalance of costs rewards, or a high number of risk factors

E Ending — Deterioration may lead the couple to end the relationship

Stern's Four-Stage Model: Stern's four-stage relationship model, developed by marketing researcher and professor Barbara Stern, was based on Levinger and Snoek's five-stage relationship development cycle and adapted to fit Stern's theory of advertising intimacy. Of the original five stages (Acquaintance, Build-up, Continuation, Dissolution, and Ending), Stern removed the "Ending" stage, thinking that departed customers are too expensive or difficult to reacquaint. The purpose of this model was to conceptualize relationship marketing, or marketing focused on customer loyalty and long-term engagement.[70]

Stern asserted that the goal of relationship marketing was to move away from impersonal mass communication and toward representations of personal disclosure. She adapted Levinger and Snoek's model for relationship development in order to study the brand/consumer relationship as a more personal, intimate process, and explore potential opportunities for improvement for advertisers. Stern gave examples of how marketing tactics could be used within this relationship model, like layering personal relevance with ambiguity to spark curiosity (Acquaintance), or reward programs and loyalty incentives (Continuity).[71]

Reis and Shaver's Interpersonal Process Model of Intimacy: H.T. Reis and P. Shaver's Interpersonal Process Model of Intimacy explains how intimacy is formed between two people, and consists of two key components: self-disclosure and partner responsiveness. The model suggests that intimacy is initiated when one person communicates personally relevant and revealing information to another. This can be factual information, personal thoughts or feelings, and may also include other means of communicating emotions through non-verbal cues, like gazing or touching. As the intimacy process moves forward, the listener in turn must respond to the speaker by disclosing similarly personally revealing information, expressing emotion, and giving non-verbal signals. As these interactions continue, intimacy is built between the two people.[72]

Reis and Shaver found that both self-disclosure and partner responsiveness contribute to the experience of intimacy. Two studies tested this model and strongly supported the conceptualization of intimacy as a combination of self-disclosure and partner disclosure at the level of individual interactions, with partner responsiveness serving as a partial mediator in this process. (Interestingly, the second study also found that self-disclosure of emotion was even *more* of an important predictor of intimacy than self-disclosure of facts and information.[73])

Although this model was designed to explain the development process of interpersonal intimacy, it has been adapted to study relationships between marketers and consumers. Because it identifies perceived partner responsiveness as an important element of building intimacy, it suggests that marketers can build stronger consumer relationships by showing that they are responsive to consumers' thoughts and needs.[74]

Andrea Scott's Adaptations: In Andrea Diahann Gaye Scott's study of intimacy in services marketing, she adapts Stern's four-stage relationship cycle, as well as Reis and Shaver's Intimacy Process Model, to better fit her study of the consumer-marketer relationship. Scott advances Stern's adaptation of the Levinger and Snoek model by adding relevant marketing constructs to contextualize each of the stages: Acquaintance becomes [Involvement], Build-up becomes [Risk], Continuation, [Satisfaction], Dissolution, [Loyalty; Voice], and Ending is [Negative Word of Mouth].[75]

In addition to adapting and expanding these models, Scott also identified three advertising appeals (rational, warmth, and intimacy) and outlined the differences between them in order to study how they affect the consumer-advertiser relationship. For each, she sought to identify the focus of the ad, the creative strategy, the creative execution, the creative components, the primary processing mode, the desired consumer outcome, and the impact of individual differences.[76]

DESCRIPTIVE COMPARISON OF RATIONAL, WARMTH AND INTIMACY APPEALS

	Rational	Warmth	Intimacy
1. Focus of Ad	Product/Service offering	Emotions associated with product/service	Relationships associated with product/service
2. Creative Strategy	Emphasizes facts	Emphasizes feelings	Balances facts and feelings
3. Creative Execution	Touts the attributes of the offering	Relies heavily on peripheral cues (e.g. soft music, cozy images)	Reveals personal (and emotional) information
4. Creative Components	Prices/related APR's Company reputation	Fond memories afforded by service Company involvement	Discreetly discloses unknown information Company concern and commitment
5. Primary Processing Mode	Cognitive	Affective	Both Cognitive and Affective
6. Desired Consumer Outcome	Knowledge	Liking and "warm fuzzies"	Bonding
7. Impact of Individual Differences	Little to none	Moderate	High
8. Market Example	American Express: "Don't leave home without it"	Hallmark: "When you care enough to send the very best"	State Farm Insurance: "We live where you live"

Chart of Andrea Diahann Gaye Scott's Advertising Appeal Construct

THE FORMS OF INTIMACY

From these more theoretical constructs, we move to Beverly Golden, a writer and cultural purveyor, who has further dimensioned the "faces" or forms of intimacy. The most obvious is a physical or sexual connotation, although even this form has more nuance. People want to feel safe while being vulnerable, and this form of intimacy also includes a wide range of sensuous activity and sensual expression.

Emotional intimacy, by contrast, happens when two people feel comfortable sharing their feelings with each other. Fears related to this, which include the fear of rejection (losing the other person) and the fear of engulfment (being invaded, controlled, and losing oneself) can sometimes inhibit or prevent the development of intimacy.

Intellectual or cognitive intimacy is about communication—the ability to share ideas in an open and comfortable way, which can lead to a very intimate relationship.

Finally, there is experiential intimacy, or intimacy of activity, the essence of which is that very little need be said to each other. It's not a verbal sharing of thoughts or feelings, but it's more about involving yourself in an activity and feeling an intimacy from this involvement.[77]

THE FORMS OF INTIMACY

Name	Description	Outcome
Physical	A sensual or sexual connection	Feeling of physical unity
Emotional	The mutual sharing of innermost feelings	Feeling of being understood and accepted as an individual
Cognitive	An exchange of ideas and exploration of similarities and differences in them	Feeling of intellectual connection
Experiential	Involvement in an activity that produces shared behaviors	Feeling of being part of a special group: togetherness, camaraderie, being in sync

IN CONCLUSION

Reviewing various definitions and approaches to building intimacy provided important perspectives on the power of emotions and the closeness experienced by those in intimate relationships.

While there are multiple approaches detailing intimacy between people, we saw little thinking around the possibility of being intimate with brands.

1-5

DISCOVERY

Our quest to find answers related to creating a new marketing paradigm was a comprehensive and insightful one. It began with a broad investigation into how the marketing of yesterday has been transformed into the selling of today. We wanted to understand what businesses were doing to address current realities to help them achieve growth. We also wanted to review relevant marketing models and methodologies, to gain a richer perspective on what was being recommended by the best and the brightest. We read books, articles, and research studies on how changes in brands and technology are impacting the modern consumer. We assessed multiple theories, models, and doctrines from psychologists, scientists, and economists, all who have published on topics related to the science of decision making. We then moved into our extensive study on the psychology of intimacy, looking to understand historic and academic approaches.

All of this got us excited about what we felt was a better way to measure, build and manage brands. We hadn't yet completely concretized our thinking; however, we knew that we were heading in the right direction—and that no one to our knowledge had yet connected the dots and put forward an approach that leveraged all this information.

First, we wanted to test our theory about the ability of people to form intimate relationships with brands and get firsthand knowledge. This required learning directly from consumers about if, how, why and when they form attachments to brands.

Working with a very similarly-minded research firm, BrainJuicer (now System1), we developed an intensive eight-week online community of consumers from the United States, Germany, and Japan. Respondents were first questioned about relationships in their lives, how they form intimacy with people, how they feel about intimacy, if and how they form relationships with brands, and what brands they've been very close to. We wanted to better understand how people interact with brands in their everyday lives, why they feel close to certain brands (but not others), how they talk about these brands, and what characteristics or attributes they ascribe to them. We also wanted to learn about the longevity of these relationships. Do people break up with brands? Once established, do these relationships last forever?

QUALITATIVE RESEARCH
20,000 STORIES

350
CONSUMERS

10 **WEEKS**
1,000 **HOURS**

We amassed over 20,000 unique stories from more than 350 people, which resulted in 2,000 pages of data, based on 1,000 hours of insights. In addition to our insight communities, we completed an online content analysis through an algorithm created to search queries for 110 keywords, identified from our insight communities, across three contexts: personal, social, and environmental, looking on blogs, social networks and communities.

It took months to pour through this data, reading stories in full, synthesizing key information, identifying patterns, and detailing some frameworks. Nine key findings from this research helped shape our understanding and became the core of our thinking on brand intimacy.

FINDINGS:

1/9

BRAND INTIMACY PARALLELS
HUMAN INTIMACY

This was an important insight, and confirmed our thinking about people and brands. Could brand and human relationships really be that similar? Our assumption was that people do indeed have strong attachments to certain brands, but we couldn't be sure if it was to the same degree as personal connections, and if so, how similar the process was. But in fact, intimate brand relationships do appear to closely mirror intimate human relationships.

People have a standard way in which they develop significant relationships, be it with another person or a brand, and they can form real and deep attachments to brands the way they do with people. The steps are similar, the processes the same, and the outcomes aligned.

I think of intimacy as a more
intense brand relationship.

German consumer

I develop a feeling for a company or brand or
product that is similar to love. It is beyond a
cold business relationship because the brand
has become inseparable from myself.

Japanese consumer

Audi is practically a member of the family.

German consumer

FINDINGS:

2/9

BRAND INTIMACY MIMICS
FORMS OF HUMAN INTIMACY

Not only does brand intimacy parallel human intimacy, but the forms and types of intimacy also align quite strongly.

Writer and cultural purveyor Beverly Golden created the Faces or Forms of Intimacy, which directly correlates to the ways consumers describe the types of brand intimacy they experience. Obviously, because brands are inanimate constructs (generally speaking), the sexual aspect of physical intimacy is less relevant. However, there are numerous ways that brands can foster closeness through sensorial stimulation. Consider some of the ways that Starbucks, for example, engages the senses: the store's design and layout (sight), the music played in the store (sound), the aroma of the coffee (smell), the warmth of the cup of coffee in your hand (touch), and the distinctive flavor of the coffee (taste).

Four Forms
of Intimacy

Brand Intimacy
Manifestation

COGNITIVE
An exchange of
ideas and exploration
of similarities or
differences in them

Stimulating passionate
agreement and
dedication to a
distinctive and
compelling idea, sense
of purpose or ethos

EMOTIONAL
The mutual sharing of
innermost feelings

Eliciting feelings of
being understood and
accepted as an individual
through personalized
engagement

PHYSICAL
A sensual or sexual
connection

Sensual and sensorial
stimulation that provides
pleasurable and
gratifying feelings

EXPERIENTIAL
Involvement in an
activity that produces
shared experiences

Engaging people socially,
including them in an
exclusive group to create
feelings of togetherness,
camaraderie and
belonging

PHYSICAL INTIMACY

Aligns to a sensorial-oriented relationship between a consumer and a brand that develops through engagement of the senses. Brands that we ingest (e.g., food and drink) as well as brands used/worn on or near the body are often associated with physical aspects of intimacy.

"

I found Wen cleansing conditioner
almost two years ago and have only used
that product to clean my hair. They use a
blend of herbs and natural ingredients instead
of harsh chemicals that strip your hair of
its natural oils. Beside the benefits of using
all-natural ingredients, the amazing scent
gives you a wonderful aromatherapy session
every morning in the shower.

U.S. consumer

EMOTIONAL INTIMACY

Links to a deeply personal relationship between a consumer and a brand that develops because the consumer feels understood and accepted as an individual. While brands may not have innermost feelings to share, brands can still create emotional intimacy through the projection of emotion, which they do in many ways, and by eliciting emotional responses in consumers. Consider how many sports brands inspire consumers through imagery that projects the exhilaration of athletic achievement.

Often, emotional intimacy is manifested by a brand through thoughtful gestures and a caring nature.

For me, it is all about caring. Because
I'm so endeared to Southwest, I want them
to succeed even though I have no direct
relationship. I want the company to do well,
I want the employees to be happy,
I want their safety record to be spotless—
everything that causes a company to
surpass others, I wish for them.

U.S. consumer

COGNITIVE INTIMACY

Emphasizes a more reason-based relationship between a consumer and a brand that develops around a feeling of intellectual connection, often centered on a deep level of affinity and respect for the brand's values or ethos.

"

I feel that brand-intimate companies have different values than those that aren't brand-intimate. I feel that brand-intimate brands are more customer-focused. They are more interested in pleasing the customer over the bottom line and are more likely to provide quality services or products. They value customers.

U.S. consumer

"

EXPERIENTIAL INTIMACY

Fosters a socially focused relationship between a consumer and a brand that develops through a feeling of being part of a special group.

"

Samsung is an electronics genius and very popular with our family. We consider ourselves to be 'of the Samsung tribe.' Everyone has the latest generation of Samsung: TV, landline phone, mobile phone—everything from Samsung, precisely because it is very reliable.

German consumer

FINDINGS:

3/9

RECIPROCITY IS KEY

Further echoing the structure of human relationships, reciprocity is key when it comes to developing strong brand connections. Two-way engagement is essential; both brand and person must be active participants. Consumers may choose to deepen communication with brands by opting in for emails, signing up for newsletters, and filling out warranty cards. Some will begin a more active brand conversation through liking brands on Facebook, replying to posts, and sharing branded content. Yet it is exceedingly rare to read any marketing strategies or theories that discuss this two-way reciprocal nature of a brand relationship, so this is a new and important way to think about building bonds.

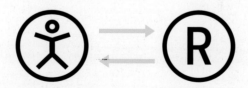

Midori milk and Miyoshi soap bring health and happiness to my family and children. They nurture us, so I feel close to the brand—like it's a family member.

Japanese consumer

4/9

SIX MAIN ARCHETYPES
DELIVER BRAND INTIMACY

We observed how people explained and defined their close brand relationships, and over and over the same types of words and experiences were used to explain the bond a person felt with a brand. The more we reviewed these, the more we realized these markers were among the most effective tools to leverage in building brand intimacy. Software helped us determine frequency and later factor analysis was used to prioritize, combine and summarize groupings of sentiment, feelings and associations.

We detailed six archetypes that are consistently present, in part or in whole, among intimate brands. These help identify the character and nature of intimate brand relationships. Interestingly, we found a brand can be intimate across more than one archetype, and global brands can be associated with different archetypes in different countries. For example, German consumers are twice as likely as Americans or Japanese consumers to engage with brands via the nostalgia archetype. Japanese consumers are significantly more likely to form intimate brand relationships based on the identity archetype, while Mexican consumers have the highest rates of indulgence.

Brand Archetypes

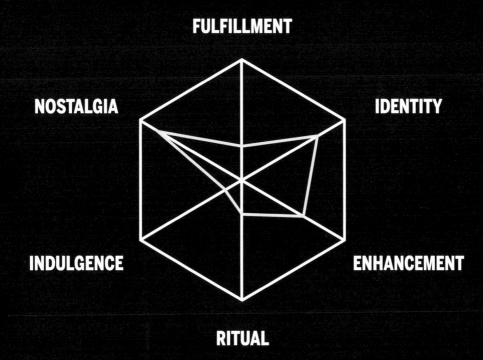

FULFILLMENT

NOSTALGIA

IDENTITY

INDULGENCE

ENHANCEMENT

RITUAL

Indicates Brand
Performance

"

FULFILLMENT   I only buy Tide and I rarely look at other brands of laundry detergent. I think it works the best. I get the best results with Tide; I must have eight bottles of it at any given time in my laundry room.

U.S. consumer

IDENTITY   Apple products are easy to use, stylish and fast. They make me look modern and maybe even cool.

U.S. consumer

ENHANCEMENT   PlayStation has been there for me since I was a preteen. It was a great way to connect with my brother... I have made friends through games, learned how to problem solve, and even added accomplishing things 'in game' into my list of life achievements.

U.S. consumer

"

"

RITUAL

For me, Lavazza coffee is simply the best. Every day, the first thing I do is enjoy my Lavazza coffee. The whole thing has already become a routine, which I won't do without.

German consumer

INDULGENCE

I love Lindt for its high quality. This company manufactures its products using only the finest ingredients. This makes it a brand I love to eat and like to give as a gift on special occasions, such as Easter, birthdays, Christmas...

German consumer

NOSTALGIA

I've been fascinated with foreign music since I was a child. I bought foreign music magazines and admired the brands in those magazines. One of the brands I aspired to then was Fender guitars. I have one now, and it brings back all of my great childhood memories.

Japanese consumer

"

FINDINGS:

5/9

BRAND INTIMACY HAPPENS
IN STAGES OR PHASES

Even if you encounter a brand that you find a powerful attraction to, you don't immediately form an intimate relationship. Intimacy takes time. It requires that you build trust, interaction, commitment, and ultimately, being co-identified.

As is the case with personal relationships, our qualitative research revealed that there are specific and distinct stages one must progress through when cultivating brand intimacy. While the amount of time it takes to reach brand intimacy may vary, the three stages are consistent, regardless of brand, culture, or geography. Similar to human relationships, there is risk at every stage that the relationship could end; however, the deeper the relationship and the higher the stage it progresses to, the greater the potential for forgiveness.

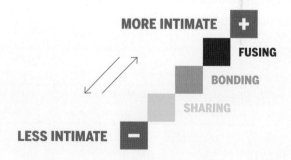

MORE INTIMATE +

FUSING

BONDING

SHARING

LESS INTIMATE −

“

FUSING

Red Valentino represents a way of life that is very important to me. Wearing them is an expression of me.

Japanese consumer

BONDING

I spend a lot of time using computers and I feel intimacy with my mouse. It has never let me down. It's is easy to use and helped me accomplish a lot of things. It has also brought me a lot of delight.

Japanese consumer

SHARING

I feel like Nike understands my needs and I have a good idea what this company stands for and represents.

U.S. consumer

FINDINGS:

6/9

INTIMACY IS NOT PERMANENT
(WITHOUT WORK)

Like human relationships, even when intimacy is gained, it does not mean it lasts forever. Brands must work hard to maintain their relationships with consumers, or risk losing them. This involves everything from keeping quality levels high, adapting to consumer needs, rewarding those who are deeply involved with you, and apologizing when errors are made. Violating or betraying consumer trust can have grave consequences. We do believe, however, that when a brand relationship is intimate, there is a greater chance of forgiveness by consumers. Still, continuous grievances will inevitably result in a broken or dysfunctional relationship. The opposing state to intimacy is not rejection—but as we learned, it's indifference, which we will detail next.

"

I may be more likely to forgive minor transgressions like getting a poor quality product (once) knowing, or at least thinking, that this is not the norm for this company. If I get more than one disappointment, though, I will likely look elsewhere the next time I need a product that the company offers.

U.S. consumer

FINDINGS:

7/9

INDIFFERENCE IS THE OPPOSITE OF INTIMACY

We identified through reading consumer stories detailing their brand relationships that the opposite of intimacy is indifference. This comes after temporary feelings like anger and frustration have dissipated. Indifference is a sense of irrelevance, feelings of apathy and detachment, or being aloof and disinterested. It can happen at any stage of the journey toward intimacy and is a risk that needs to be considered at all times. Brand relationships, like human relationships, are never static. They are in a constant state of flux, moving closer together or further apart.

Nothing hurts a brand more than bad quality and disappointment in product/ service performance. When a brand is not reliable in a consumer's own experience, it spells trouble. This can undo years of goodwill because the brand is no longer delivering on the most basic attributes of functionality and reliability. See section 3.2 Failures, Perspectives and Lessons for more insights on indifference.

Failing to evolve can also increase the chance of indifference. Brands that rest on their laurels based on former successes and miss opportunities to develop further will oftentimes find a dearth of loyal consumers.

The brand just failed me too many times to remain a valued part of my life.

U.S. consumer

I've outgrown a few brands.
They didn't change with the times.

U.S. consumer

8/9

BRAND INTIMACY IS RARE

Today brand intimacy is limited and not common. During our initial screening process to find appropriate research respondents, nearly 4,000 consumers were considered. Among them, less than one quarter of people demonstrated the potential of having brand-intimate relationships. In addition, the pool of intimate consumers is reduced further given the fact that one must be a user of the brand to be considered for inclusion. The percentage of intimate users increased later in our quantitative research; however, it's not surprising given that there has been little concerted effort up to this point regarding building intimate brands.

"

These brands all make products
that I use, but I don't have an intimate
relationship with any of them.

U.S. consumer

I wouldn't say I'm intimate
with any brand.

German consumer

9/9

TECHNOLOGY ENABLES—BUT ALSO CAN DIMINISH—BRAND INTIMACY

While technology can facilitate brand intimacy, it can also harm or end the relationship; it's a double-edged sword. Most consumers seem to take for granted that brands use technology to reach them. People are talking to brands, brands are communicating to them, people are talking to each other about brands... this engagement is going on 24 hours a day, whenever and wherever you are. That has fundamentally changed the methods brands have to engage people and create close relationships.

Technology also reveals a downside, such as when a brand communicates to you in a way that is uninvited, or feels obtrusive or intrusive. When that happens, it actually pushes consumers further away. Marketers must find the sweet spot between annoying and meaningful communication. They must also do a good job of managing any data they are privileged to receive. This includes protecting privacy and not leaking consumer information to other parties.

"

I think the interactions you have either with email or a website can really affect how you feel about the brand.

Japanese consumer

The ideal brand would use technology to establish a regular communication channel with me. This would usually be email, and offer regular rewards for my loyalty, provide an easy way for me to submit feedback and give the brand an opportunity to show an appreciation for my feedback.

U.S. consumer

These nine findings framed our understanding of how people form intimate relationships with brands. Reading detailed explanations and 20,000 stories from consumers about their feelings, connections and bonds with products, services and companies provided invaluable insights. From there, we moved to concretize the idea and model data to quantify the mechanisms and drivers of intimate relationships.

Key Findings:

1. **BRAND INTIMACY PARALLELS HUMAN INTIMACY**

2. **BRAND INTIMACY MIMICS FORMS OF HUMAN INTIMACY**

3. **RECIPROCITY IS KEY**

4. **SIX MAIN ARCHETYPES DELIVER BRAND INTIMACY**

5. **BRAND INTIMACY HAPPENS IN STAGES OR PHASES**

6. **INTIMACY IS NOT PERMANENT (WITHOUT WORK)**

7. **INDIFFERENCE IS THE OPPOSITE OF INTIMACY**

8. **BRAND INTIMACY IS RARE**

9. **TECHNOLOGY ENABLES—BUT ALSO CAN DIMINISH—BRAND INTIMACY**

IMPLICATIONS

Brands have tremendous impact and the capacity to build powerful bonds.

90 percent of decisions we make are driven by emotion.

The democratization of brand today, the role of technology, and advances in neuroscience have dramatically altered marketing and commerce.

Established marketing approaches and models, while valuable, do not reflect new market forces or consider the important role emotion plays in brand building.

Intimacy and intimate relationships are a compelling new way to examine and explore the consumer-brand dynamic.

People form relationships with brands the same way they develop relationships with other people.

2

THEORY & MODEL

Dimensioning and detailing the components of brand intimacy and how we got there provides tangible answers as to why we need a new marketing paradigm and the importance of leveraging emotions.

2-1

DEFINITION AND MODEL

BRAND INTIMACY DEFINITION AND MODEL

When defining brand intimacy, the explanation that left the biggest impression was Erik Erikson's articulation of intimacy—that "intimacy is the ability to fuse your identity with someone else's without the fear that you're going to lose something yourself."[78] This felt significant because it identifies two elements that are essential to understanding brand intimacy:

Sense of Security: This describes the lack of fear, or the sense of security people develop in a relationship through experiences over time that enable them to let their guard down and be more open to sharing.

Sense of Fulfillment: The idea of fused identities describes a relationship in which there is a close personal connection and a feeling of belonging together.

This core definition served as our foundation. We then wanted to further our approach by creating a model to build and measure brand intimacy.

This started with our online communities and initial thinking, and then was deepened through extensive quantitative research. In total, we have conducted research with more than 12,000 consumers in the U.S., Mexico, the UAE, Japan and Germany. We have read over 20,000 qualitative brand stories and interpreted more than 100,000 quantitative brand evaluations.

The quantitative survey was designed to complement and extend our previous qualitative work. We wanted to further understand the extent to which consumers have relationships with brands and the strength of those relationships across a variety of industries. We also wanted to see which brands excelled at creating intimacy with their customers. Through factor analysis, structural equation modeling, and other analytic techniques, this research enabled us to identify which dimensions need to be leveraged to build intimacy between brands and consumers most effectively.

The Brand Intimacy Model comprises key components that contribute toward building intimate brand relationships. It was developed based on the understanding that the world around us has drastically changed, and leverages the knowledge that emotions play a fundamental role in our decision making. While proposing that brands have an emotional component is not new, establishing a new approach built on emotion and intimacy is.

The model builds on the fact that you must be a user of the brand to be intimate. Anyone who has a strong emotional connection with a brand has already passed through a series of earlier, more introductory phases (which pre-date actually forming a relationship) including things like awareness, consideration, preference, and purchase. Thus, brand intimacy is a more select and advanced approach, already assuming a relationship exists.

Let's review the Brand Intimacy Model in more detail.

BRAND INTIMACY:

BRAND INTIMACY IS
A NEW PARADIGM THAT
LEVERAGES AND STRENGTHENS
THE EMOTIONAL BONDS
BETWEEN
A PERSON AND A BRAND

HOW WE MEASURE BRAND INTIMACY

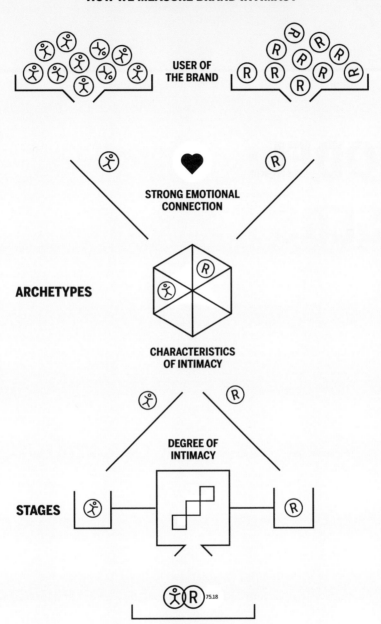

USER OF THE BRAND

STRONG EMOTIONAL CONNECTION

ARCHETYPES

CHARACTERISTICS OF INTIMACY

DEGREE OF INTIMACY

STAGES

BRAND INTIMACY QUOTIENT

2-2

MODEL: USERS

The user is the first component in our model. It is a critical part and already different from most other approaches, which generally are broader in their focus. To be intimate with a brand, you need to have repeatedly tried it or used it. Intimacy presupposes consumers are already aware and familiar with a brand. Think of this in terms of human relationships; to be intimate with someone, you must already be involved with them. Because the very nature of intimacy presupposes a relationship, and usually a significant one, our model is by necessity more specific and more elevated. This ensures that the way we look at, rank, and diagnose brands is based on those people who are already involved and in some form of intimacy. While what constitutes a user will vary depending on the audiences of individual brands, this is our non-negotiable starting point: you must already be a user of the brand to be considered intimate in any way.

In addition to being a user of a brand, having a strong emotional connection to the brand is also required. Emotional connection is at the heart of brand intimacy and aligns with all we've learned about decision making from neuro-science and behavioral science. Very few models address emotion and even fewer make it a core component. Emotion is everything. It leads, focuses and motivates our decisions. The more people feel, the more it impacts their relationship to brands. To start an intimate brand relationship, a consumer must exhibit a strong emotional connection with a brand. Not everyone who has an emotional connection with a brand is necessarily intimate with it; however, everyone who is intimate with a brand has a strong emotional connection. The greater the emotional connection between a brand and consumer, the more powerful the relationship. A strong emotional connection is determined by the degree of overall positive feelings a customer has toward a brand and the extent to which a person associates the brand with key attributes. We asked respondents in our quantitative survey to describe how they felt about brands in terms of having a strong emotional connection, a positive relationship, neutral feelings or negative associations. Only those with positive and strong feelings would proceed to evaluate the brand further.

Why is this so important? Definitions of intimacy require a strong emotional connection. For example, Sharon Brehm, former president of the American Psychological Association, who notes, "The defining characteristics of an inti-mate relationship are one or more of the following: behavioral interdependence, need fulfillment, and emotional attachment."[79]

2-3

MODEL: ARCHETYPES

Brand archetypes appeal to individual psyches; they help us to make sense of the world and identify patterns and connections that can lead to intimacy. Psychologist Carl Jung theorized that people have a tendency to use symbolism to understand and process concepts. And while our brand archetypes are similar, in that they are markers and cues, it is important to reiterate that we did not invent these archetypes nor are they arbitrary. They were observed, self described and summarized by consumers when detailing their brand relationships in our qualitative research, and later validated by our quantitative factor analysis.

Archetypes are important because they are a unique lens or filter on brand associations. They represent our fundamental needs and desires; they are shortcuts that can bring us closer to brands. Since people are driven by instincts and are emotional decision makers, archetypes are the key initial ingredient to building more intimate brands.

We discovered six patterns or markers are consistently present, in part or in whole, among intimate relationships. They identify the nature and character of these relationships. Structural equation modeling from our quantitative research then revealed how these six archetypes drive the intensity of the relationship between consumers and brands. The brands that are most effective at fostering intimate relationships do a great job embracing or adopting one or more of these archetypes. Since we know that brands need to connect with consumers quickly and instinctively, archetypes also provide an effective shorthand to build bonds and form attachments.

This idea is not dissimilar from Christopher Booker's thesis in *The Seven Basic Plots*, which suggests that all stories follow seven basic themes, that stories mirror psychological development, and that we process information in an instinctive and primal way.[80]

What does this mean for brands? In brief, it means that it is advantageous to understand what a brand's underlying story is. It means that relating your brand to as many archetypes as makes sense is a good thing; that these anchors create powerful territories for brands to express themselves and be identified with. By understanding the impact of each archetype, marketers can better determine what levers to push to more effectively move brands from indifference to intimacy. Archetypes help ensure you have an emotional component as part of your brand's DNA.

Archetypes are the foundational elements to the bonds that we form with brands. They are the glue that attracts and connects. Each is unique, powerful and fundamental to how brands can thrive. Here, we'll dive deeper into better understanding them by dimensioning each through real examples. You'll see that a brand doesn't necessarily need to think of archetypes as overt or literal messaging or a campaign; rather, think of them as ways to imbue or orient the relationship between brand and people. For each brand selected from our rankings, we'll explore a detailed view of their brand performance and the role that these archetypes play in helping them achieve stronger bonds with customers.

ARCHETYPES:

FULFILLMENT

ALWAYS EXCEEDS EXPECTATIONS

DELIVERS SUPERIOR QUALITY/SERVICE

GOOD VALUE FOR THE MONEY

amazon

"

Amazon Prime is incredible; I can't imagine our life without it. Anything we need it just appears like magic and if there is ever a problem—they just fix it.

U.S. consumer

I consider my relationship to Amazon intimate, because they are able to fulfill my wishes.

U.S. consumer

"

Fulfillment is about exceeding expectations and being reliable. For Amazon, it means much more. The Amazon brand has not only built a unique business proposition (a combination of retail, cloud services, entertainment, and technology); it also dominates our brand intimacy rankings. But if we asked you to think about the warm and fuzzy attributes the Amazon brand connotes, could you name any? Probably not.

So how does it perform so well in driving what ultimately matters most—how consumers feel about the brand? Unquestionably, it is a successful business, with the brand valued at nearly $70 billion, a 24 percent increase from 2015.[81] Is it performing some brand "mind tricks'" that have been concocted in its labs (along with drone delivery squadrons)? Can any retail brand, online or otherwise, catch Amazon? What drives its unique blend of brand performance?

To understand this, let's bear in mind that Amazon leads our retail category, and is a top three overall ranking brand that has fast risen across our study. Amazon leads its category in the fulfillment archetype. At first blush, this seems both obvious and basic—a table stakes requirement for a business in online retailing. However, exceeding expectations and being reliable provides confidence, trust, and assurance. These are all critical in building bonds and deepening relationships. Delivering or over-delivering on expectations for a brand can take the basics of "good service" to a whole other level. Brands that innovate in this space enjoy the benefits of becoming verbs in our everyday vocabulary (e.g., Google). Fulfillment is a popular archetype with many of the top-ranked brands, across many industries in our study. It is also perhaps the broadest archetype, compared to more focused alternates like indulgence or nostalgia, suggesting that in order to master it, a brand must do many things well. For Amazon, this resonates with their operational efficiency and technological prowess.

As an online retail pioneer, Amazon provides fulfillment by simultaneously obsessing narrowly over every pixel of the customer journey to broadly expanding the ecosystem of influence and boundaries of what you can effortlessly buy and have shipped to your door. Amazon is fearless, innovative, and consistently trying to improve their offerings in ways big and small. This experience drives feelings of confidence and trust among Amazon's customers.

Amazon leads on fulfillment through superior service by being reliable, anticipatory, and most importantly, consistently offering value (savings). By knowing its customers' profiles and suggesting appropriate items, it gains traction. By delivering flawlessly, it creates an addictive pleasure. By offering a truly unmatched roster of products, it's convenient, and it exceeds expectations by continually innovating, evolving, and expanding its offerings. Through mastering logistics and the supply chain, Amazon can disintermediate how products arrive in its customers' hands. Amazon Prime further motivates customers with a new kind of loyalty that provides discounts on delivery (both time and money), as well as offering entertainment options and other savings. It's working; Amazon Prime customers spend an average of $1,500 a year with Amazon, compared to non-Prime members who spend $625.[82]

The brand doesn't talk fulfillment, it embodies it, through every aspect of how Amazon is experienced, enjoyed and delivered. This is an important contribution, as it suggests archetypes should not be considered purely along communication platforms. Rather, they can be thought of as behaviors or pillars of a brand, and experienced through usage.

You can see a chart showing our top-ranked retail brands (in order of ranking) and their archetype scores for fulfillment. Amazon leads the field, and about half the top 10 brands are at or below the industry average for this critical category archetype.

FULFILLMENT ARCHETYPE PERFORMANCE BY RETAIL BRAND

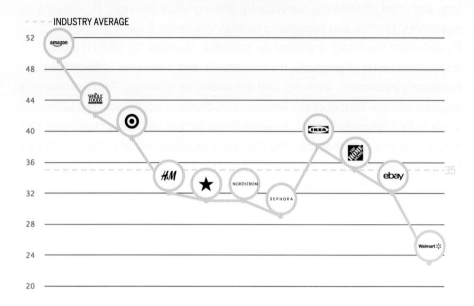

We've also discovered those retail brands that score well in fulfillment (the retail category archetype driver) generally have a larger percentage of fusing-stage relationships with their customers. Thus, a strong performance in this archetype clearly links to developing intimate relationships. Amazon has the highest percentage of fusing customers (those in the highest stage of intimacy) among retail brands and ranks fourth out of nearly all 200 brands in our survey for having the largest percentage of fusing customers.

PERCENTAGE OF FUSING CUSTOMERS BY RETAIL BRAND

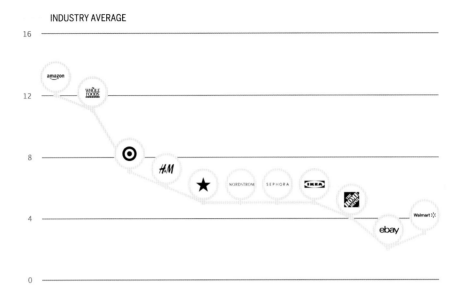

Amazon is winning in brand intimacy by building stronger bonds with its customers, and that bodes well for its future success. Amazon outperforms the category on fulfillment, which has helped drive an impressive 51 percent of its customers to experience some form of intimacy with the brand. By comparison, the category average is 34 percent (see next chart).

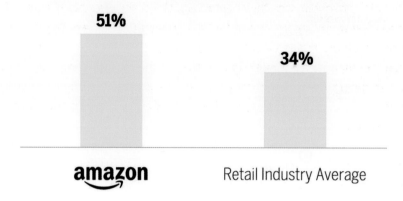

PERCENTAGE OF CUSTOMERS IN STAGES OF INTIMACY

51%

amazon

34%

Retail Industry Average

Amazon also ranks second in our research as the favorite brand of millennials (18–34-year-olds) and first among those who make $35,000–100,000 per year. The brand dominates the average retailers in frequency of use and has almost double the average price resilience. It also scores highly for customers on the measure "Can't Live Without." If that isn't convincing enough, note that Amazon is trusted more than any other online retailer,[83] that it invested nearly $10 billion last year in R&D,[84] and that its cloud services division will soon eclipse the operating profit of its retail business,[85] and you can quickly see that its dominance is only beginning. Like most large companies ($50 billion in revenues and counting), there is no simple or singular explanation for Amazon's success. It is rare, however, to see such brand strength from a company that seems to do so little to articulate itself from a marketing and communication perspective. When was the last time you saw an Amazon advertisement?

Amazon continues to defy brand conventions in other ways, too. In general, brands have a more difficult time moving from a value positioning to a luxury or valued one. Compounding this challenge, brands that fulfill utility functions are further susceptible to being marginalized. Once brands are relegated to this base level association, it is extremely difficult for them to rise up in associations with consumers. Cell phone providers, utilities (like power), or even your TV cable company, are examples of the type of brands that typically have low emotional connections with their customers. Often we see a high degree of trapped loyalist customers—those that continue to use the service yet feel trapped or without options to switch. Reflecting on Amazon, though there isn't any really comparable competition of scale and they deliver utility-like service (online shopping and delivery), they don't create consumers who feel like trapped loyalists. Even more impressive is that they continue to add a broad array of products and services, ranging from personal electronics, enter-tainment, and content to enterprise cloud services, all of which are currently meeting with market success. Their brand seems to defy the boundaries of what is traditionally possible or considered a best practice.

By being pervasive, direct, and peerless in fulfilling customer needs, Amazon has established itself as essential to its customers. Its dominance in fulfillment is clearly part of its success. It has become a new brand staple in people's lives, something upon which they depend. Although it does not appear to promote emotionally oriented brand messaging or advertising, the Amazon brand, indeed, has anchored itself squarely in the hearts of its users, becoming a brand they feel connected to and that they count on.

Brand intimacy and Amazon? Most definitely.

ARCHETYPES:

IDENTITY

I ASPIRE TO…

HAS VALUES I STRONGLY IDENTIFY WITH

HELPS ME PROJECT A DESIRABLE LIFESTYLE

"

Whole Foods...I love the adventure of seeing what's new and healthy and interesting. I connect with this brand and what it stands for.

U.S. consumer

Whole Foods is among the brands that do the best job of creating intimate relationships with people. They consistently provide top quality goods. They are not just four walls where you go buy something. They believe in sustainability and health. So do I.

U.S. consumer

"

A more "authentic" brand is a very desirable attribute. Wonder why that is? Or why authentic, real experiences resonate strongly with consumers? These attributes are central to the archetype we call identity. The identity archetype is most prevalent in brands that have a strong purpose or belief system. These brands typically strive for a high-order benefit to underpin their essence or reason for being. Often, these brands prioritize their commitment to values over share value. Consider the commitment and powerful identification of brands like Ben & Jerry's or The Body Shop to social and environmental causes. The Johnson & Johnson credo is another pioneering example of how a company can define itself through holistic business and brand beliefs.

The identity archetype is the most classic of archetypes, in terms of aligning to our traditional understanding of brands standing for something aspirational and compelling. Brands that leverage identity tend to be confident and proud. Clarity in what the company does and does not stand for is key to communicating a focused and authentic message that is ownable within and across industries.

The other component of the identity archetype is aspiration. This can be combined with values that resonate or be demonstrated distinctly (Nike and Rolex are examples of brands we aspire to).

As our lives continue to increase in complexity with a barrage of technology and media messages, we've become increasingly dis-intermediated from each other. There is a growing school of thought that, with these chaotic times, belief in brands with a high purpose or values-based essence gives us something to believe in and a relationship to care about. Belief in these types of brands also offers us a way to bond and connect not only with the brand, but with other admirers of the brand over a sense of shared values. (Think of the Bernie Sanders campaign during the 2016 presidential election, where people, particularly millennials, identified clearly with the shared values Mr. Sanders was espousing. This in turn created a "movement" that has been much discussed, providing a shared cause and a clear way to identify one's self).

Now, for a real world example of identity at work. Does it surprise you to learn that according to our study, one of the top 10 ranking brick-and-mortar retail brands in the United States is Whole Foods? In 36 short years, this grocery store has established itself as the leading supermarket brand for quality, organic food, and lifestyle products. Whole Foods' commitment to fair trade and labor practices, charity, the environment, and "natural" products of high quality is well established. The brand has ranked one of "100 Best Companies to Work For" by Fortune for 18 consecutive years,[86] and its average hourly wage for full-time workers was $19.16 in fiscal year 2014.[87]

A trip to a Whole Foods gives the visitor an immediate and visceral experience of the importance that the brand places on its core values. By making sure the makeup of the products stays front and center and, where possible, the sourcing of the product itself is visible and highlighted, consumers gain both a clear signal to what the retail brand prioritizes and its affinity toward healthier, more sustainable living. The brand also educates and informs consumers, providing transparency in their supply chain, further building trust. The identity archetype is reflected even in the care and visual delight of the brand's fresh food displays. Clearly, there is a collective consumer desire to eat healthier and be healthier. Whole Foods mirrors this aspiration and makes us feel better about ourselves.

Purpose-driven brands that leverage the identity attribute are effective because they co-identify with consumers in profound and meaningful ways. We like brands we admire, brands that make us feel good for supporting them and that stand for principles we respect. Whole Foods ranked eighth overall in our study, and among women, the brand jumps to fourth overall. It generally performs well across ages and income levels. The rapid brand growth was also timed well, with consumers' growing demand for healthier foods and understanding of the effects of the types and ingredients of the foods that we eat.

Whole Foods achieves this level of intimacy because the brand is rooted in a strong purpose. What Jim Stengel would call "the ideal"—a brand that stands for something compelling to their customers.[88] He argues that brands rooted in a strong mission statement outperform their competitors and the market indices. This form of brand building is closely linked to the identity archetype.

Whole Foods scored considerably higher on identity compared to the rest of the industry. It also ranked third highest on identity compared to all brands in our study, after Apple and Harley Davidson, two iconic and aspirational brands. Also interesting is the economic equity related to the brand. Although considered a premium-priced store, more of total users said they would be willing to pay 20 percent more for the store's products versus the category average. When you ask fusing customers of Whole Foods the same question, a whopping 31 percent answer affirmatively.

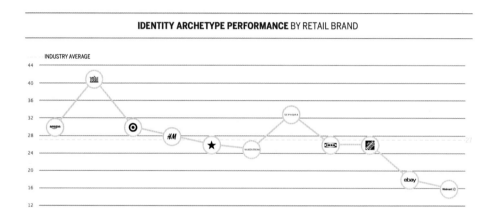

IDENTITY ARCHETYPE PERFORMANCE BY RETAIL BRAND

Interestingly when you compare this brand with Amazon, the online retailer, you see that they are dramatically different brands (almost complete opposites), yet both highly successful in their own ways. Amazon has mastered the online experience and has built an engine of convenience, quality, and reliability. Whole Foods has created a brick-and-mortar ecosystem of health, information, and transparency. Certainly with the acquisition of Whole Foods by Amazon, you see that opposites may well attract. When these two strong intimate brands align, the result may be complementary or a combination of strengths. With two very distinct intimacy profiles, it will be interesting to see how they combine forces and how that impacts the bonds they build with customers.

It is clear regardless of association or ownership that brands that link to identity must either have or establish a strong sense of who they are and find ways to make this both apparent and relevant to consumers. By nature, we find affinity with things we can easily relate to.

In other words, the more your brand identifies with and inspires your customers, the better.

ARCHETYPES:

ENHANCEMENT

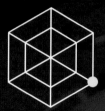

MAKES MY LIFE EASIER

HELPS ME BE MORE EFFECTIVE

MAKES ME SMARTER, MORE CAPABLE
AND MORE CONNECTED

Apple has figured out a way to be indispensable in people's lives.

Japanese consumer

Apple brings me closer to everyone and allows me to be more productive and get things done faster and easier.

U.S. consumer

Apple keeps me in touch with everyone and everything that I hold dear.

U.S. consumer

Few would be surprised to learn that Apple's brand intimacy parallels its dominant business performance. The brand ranked number one in our study, much as it leads in numerous other brand studies, product categories and overall financial returns. Apple's suite of products and their retail and online stores establish a level of overall excellence few brands can match. The brand is often the benchmark for considering best practices for academics and practitioners alike.

In our study, beyond having the highest overall quotient score (77) and top scores across the fusing stage, and "Can't Live Without" measure, the brand's most impressive performance is in achieving an extremely strong showing across five of our six archetypes. Clearly, Apple connects with consumers with several archetypes which, even on their own, can significantly help establish strong bonds; however, in combination, they have a compounding and synergistic effect.

Our focus here is primarily on how Apple leverages its most dominant archetype—enhancement—and how this archetype makes people better, smarter, more capable, and more connected. This is a high-touch archetype that is bold by definition. Even in an advancing industry like technology, Apple's enhancement score is almost 30 percent higher than the industry average.

Brands that leverage this archetype venture into a more charged territory. Deliver, and gain massive benefits; fail, and you can reach a level of indifference that can be unrecoverable for the brand. Consider the amount of scorn Apple receives whenever it produces a relatively minor or infrequent misstep, or inconveniences their customers—even if these ultimately seem to be for the consumer's own benefit. Apple has weathered a number of controversies and unhappy customers, including "Antennae Gate," the controversy over the iPhone 4's antenna causing dropped calls, which led to Consumer Reports not recommending it, and the more recent removal of the headphone jack on new iPhones in favor of a proprietary lightning connector. Weak and less intimate brands would have a much harder time weathering these sorts of customer sentiment setbacks.

From its earliest days, Apple sought to create desktop computers "for the rest of us." These first attempts to distance their brand from the likes of IBM,

Dell or Hewlett-Packard created a singular focus toward developing the very best consumer computing products on the planet. As computers became increasingly portable and merged with our entertainment and communication devices, Apple defined the leading ecosystem of hardware, software, and services for your digital life(style).

In contrast to its competitors, whose origins were in only one distinct area of computing (Microsoft, operating systems; Google, search engines; Dell/HP, hardware), Apple leveraged the ability to innovate and orchestrate the entire consumer product experience into a more seamless, cohesive software/hardware/user experience as a whole.

The category was dominated by aesthetically banal, engineering-oriented beige boxes before Apple. Apple as a company didn't just make valuable and smart products; they made beautiful ones. A computer can be elegant. A phone can be stylish. A smartwatch can be fashionable. This appreciation pervades everything about the brand. From their stores and their packaging to their marketing efforts, every decision that interfaces with the user is well considered and crafted to please. The design sensibility and attention to detail on display remains ahead, even while most of the competition has recently mimicked and followed their precedents and practices.

Apple also still looms large with the cult of personality of their founder, Steve Jobs. Dedicated to finding new, better ways for people leverage technology in their everyday lives, few brands (in fact, maybe only Google and Microsoft) can truly even begin to claim that they deliver the ability to make their users smarter, more capable, and more connected.

This is a challenging archetype to leverage; it's primarily aligned with brands that innovate and offer advanced technological capabilities. For many of us, being better and more connected relates to our devices. Those brands that are able to compellingly demonstrate the ability to make us better are rewarded for being vital to our everyday lives.

RITUAL

IS PART OF MY ROUTINE/ACTIONS

IS INGRAINED AS A VITALLY
IMPORTANT PART OF MY LIFE

MORE THAN HABITUAL BEHAVIOR

"

Starbucks coffee is simply the best for me.
Every day, the first thing I do is enjoy my
Starbucks. I connected with the brand and the
whole thing has already become a routine that
I will not do without.

Japanese consumer

At Starbucks, I know all the staff and a lot of
the customers...I am on a first name basis
there and it is like my second home and family.

U.S. consumer

I like the atmosphere in their coffee shops.
I enjoy sitting there and reading a paper while
having a drink. I feel comfortable.

German consumer

"

Ritual is a powerful archetype that aligns with brands we use frequently. Frequency appears to help build stronger bonds and keeps a brand at the top of people's minds (and hearts). Starbucks leads the fast food category in our brand intimacy study. We believe its strong performance is largely due to the ability of the brand to create a meaningful emotional connection with its customers that affects their daily behaviors, tastes, and preferences. Loyal customers (which make up 20 percent of all customers) visit Starbucks an average of 16 times a month.[89]

The brand more than doubles the weekly and daily average frequency of the category. When a consumer ingrains Starbucks into their daily actions, desire becomes need, and the brand becomes important and necessary. We believe this to be one of the most powerful and desirable archetypes in terms of building bonds, and those brands lucky enough to have ritual in their makeup have an incredible advantage. This archetype is favored by certain industries and products we use often, like cars (given the frequency with which people drive), technology (searching Google), social media brands (checking Facebook), and credit cards (paying with your Visa). In fact, we hypothesize that one of the reasons travel brands did poorly in our study may be due to their occasional usage (for most people).

Delivering a unique ethos, with their earthy and cozy interiors, the smell of fresh ground coffee, the sounds of the baristas, and curated music, it is easy to see how Starbucks delivers on their ambition to "define the third place" in our lives. Throughout its humble beginnings, the brand has continually tried to elevate the "coffee-break" into a ritualistic, pleasurable experience—an escape. With a unique vernacular for its coffee names and sizes, and a focus on an authentic vibe, Starbucks has pioneered the ability to elevate the value of a cup of joe to something closer to a religious experience. Not surprisingly, coffee bars have sprung up everywhere since Starbucks' success—though none have been quite able to catch the leader.

In our study, the brand beats the industry average in the ritual archetype combined with leading the indulgence archetype—a winning combination for a brand to become habitual, while still feeling like an indulgence. Starbucks also leverages their focus as "the third place" to further build ritual behaviors that drive intimacy.

Perhaps surprising given the comparative costs of its coffee, Starbucks performs better with lower income ranges and older age demographics. This goes to show that when a brand connects with customers in a powerful way, cost is not the deciding criteria.

Less surprising is that the brand excels with women more than men. Whether as a place to meet friends, get some work done, or simply get your morning fix, few brands can match the draw that Starbucks possesses and the behaviors in us that it affects.

Increasingly, we are seeing brands looking to better understand and affect the behaviors of their consumers. Where and how a brand intersects with those behaviors showcases some of the new and exciting thinking we see in marketing today. For brands that do own some form of ritualistic behavior, are they truly valuing and protecting it as much as they can? Given emotion's role in our decision making process, our sense of comfort and assurance formed by our habits and behaviors create a powerful advantage for brands. And for brands that are trying to embrace this archetype and affect a consumer behavior change, have you fully designed the experience to warrant the desired behavior change? How are you nurturing and fostering frequency? Do you appreciate that these aspirations are elevated and require a degree of cohesion and orchestration that may be extremely challenging to deliver? The good news for brands that do strive to achieve this rarefied level is that where there is a strong association with ritual, we often find more intimate brands.

ARCHETYPES:

NOSTALGIA

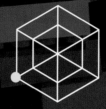

I GREW UP WITH…

REMINDS ME OF THE PAST

EVOKES MEMORIES AND THE WARM
FEELINGS I ASSOCIATE WITH THEM

LEGO, more than any other toy, brings me back to my childhood—a boundless imagination and exploration. The feel of snapping together those brightly colored blocks in endless configurations created a lifetime of positive vibes.

U.S. consumer

Brands must have a degree of legacy or history in order to draw on and leverage the powerful archetype that is nostalgia. Recent studies have shown that it proves to be a powerful marketing strategy that can promote prosocial behavior and increase consumer patience.[90] As with any of the archetypes, uninspired attempts to draw attention to or highlight the history of a company can easily be seen as kitsch or retro, in a shallow and ineffective way. This archetype goes beyond a simple throwback strategy; it must be referential without being exploitive. The secret to leveraging this archetype effectively is to fully understand and expend the potential nostalgic emotional capital available in the brand.

The LEGO brand truly stands out in its ability to draw on powerful associations from our childhood. Few brands can match the power of LEGO in terms of the nostalgia archetype. It was the highest-ranking nostalgia brand in our study in 2015 (in 2017, we didn't publish results for toy brands), outperforming the entertainment industry average not only for nostalgia, but for brand strength across all the stages (sharing, bonding, and fusing).

LEGO performs better with men than women, and with higher income levels as opposed to lower. Interestingly, it is stronger among people 18–34 than those older, even though consumer demographics data suggests that the most common purchasing category for LEGO is people 35–44.[91] For many, the nostalgic aspects and pleasure of the brand are relived when children experience the same joy of creation, reconfiguring, and rebuilding as their parents did. It's not surprising that some of their biggest partnerships make use of nostalgia-rich franchises like Star Wars, Batman, and Harry Potter. Parents like to introduce their children to things that they loved as children, and LEGO benefits from this.

Some adult LEGO fans are even buying these products for themselves; the company estimates that a little less than 5 percent of all LEGO sales are by adults that are purchasing the toys for themselves.[92] The brand has effectively used nostalgia, while also modernizing and adapting for today with more sophisticated and gender-neutral offerings. LEGO has also worked hard to create more involvement between brand and consumers, offering loyal customers more discounts and featuring customer videos on YouTube that showcase LEGO creations of all varieties.

LEGO's recent success is an incredible achievement for the brand, considering that just over a decade ago, the company was near collapse. LEGO's period of decline culminated in 2003, when it had lost 30 percent of its turnover over the past year, seeing a $240 million operating loss in sales.[93] In 2004, it began cutting costs and refocusing on its core business, and by 2006, sales were up 19 percent.[94]

At the time, every big data study that LEGO had commissioned indicated that their products would be abandoned by future generations because millennials wouldn't have the patience or time for LEGOs and would instead opt for digital toys that delivered instant gratification. However, after some more qualitative research, the LEGO team concluded that playing and developing skills were extremely valuable for attaining social currency in childhood, and that LEGO gives children of all ages a unique tool to do just that.[95] This is why LEGO plays such an important role for so many children, both socially and developmentally, and perhaps why so many adults have such strong, positive associations between the brand and childhood. LEGO provides kids with an outlet for creativity that is easy to understand, enables exploration, and produces a tangible, playable result.

Since the mid-2000s, the brand has experienced a powerful renaissance. In 2014, LEGO's sales rose 11 percent to exceed $2 billion, making it the largest toy maker in the world for the first time ever.[96] This surge was due in part to the success that *The LEGO Movie* has brought the brand, which was even further accentuated with the brand's co-opting of the 2015 Oscars. Following the song "Everything is Awesome," performers from their surprise hit movie handed out toy Oscars to A-listers who seemed to covet these statues as much as the real ones.

This is an incredible achievement for the brand, considering how a few short years ago the company was near collapse. But through focused restructuring, a broadening of product offer, a focus on the educational aspect of the brand's image and a powerful set of brand partnerships, the brand is now thriving.[97] In fact, LEGO replaced Ferrari as Brand Finance's "world's most powerful brand" in 2015.[98]

ARCHETYPES:

INDULGENCE

A PERSONAL LUXURY

MAKES ME FEEL GRATIFIED OR PAMPERED

PLEASING TO TASTE, TOUCH, SEE, SMELL, OR HEAR

SEPHORA

Nothing can cheer me up like some retail therapy at Sephora...online or off.

U.S. consumer

This brand is intimate to me because they sell products in a meaningful category to me (beauty), in a meaningful way (highly customized), they save me money and they offer luxury and excitement throughout the year(s).

U.S. consumer

One of the surprises in our study was the performance of Sephora, the beauty products retailer. Though relatively new in the United States (the first store opened in the U.S. in 1998),[99] the brand's intimacy score ranks it in the top 50 overall, seventh in retail, and first in its category for the indulgence archetype. As one might expect, the brand ranks highly among female consumers; it is the second highest retail brand among women aged 25–34 and generally performs better with younger audiences and lower income brackets. More impressively, the brand scores extremely high in the indulgence archetype, exceeding the performance of other retail brands, as well as all brands in the health and hygiene category.

Certain products and services link to indulgence more than others (as is the case with almost all the archetypes). For example, use of this archetype is frequent in food, beauty brands or luxury brands. Status images, giant product shots, and staged scenes, while common, may not be the optimal way to connect on an emotional level. Brands who leverage indulgence may want to think about ways to reframe this important archetype to build better, stronger emotional bonds.

Enter Sephora, with its ability to essentially take the department store makeup counters and create a more self-serve and focused experience. By combining hundreds of brands (as well as shaping many of their own), Sephora has given women the ability to focus their attention across the spectrum of beauty care products and beyond the family of any one brand. What's more, the store staff is well known for offering recommendations and providing information and creating an environment of positive excitement. A recent study found 90 percent of women say visiting Sephora is a highly anticipated event.[100] The brand caters to the indulgence of beauty by offering an upbeat experience complete with samples, stylish displays, and the glorification of pampering.

Therein lies the power of the Sephora brand. It trumps beauty brands by giving consumers the opportunity to cross product lines and sample multiple brands for different aspects of their beauty regimen. For more than seven decades, women in the United States have been fed a steady diet of marketing by cosmetic and beauty product brands. Some of the most iconic advertising of the Madison Avenue era can be attributed to this category alone. From "Avon calling" to the infamous Enjoli perfume ("I can bring home the bacon, fry it up in the air and never never let you forget you're a man…"), products have built and maintained a strong bond with their consumers. The concept of "I'm a Clinique woman" or "I only wear MAC cosmetics" became well-formed behavior, and historically, most women did not mix and match beauty products. Perhaps this is why 87 percent of women said Sephora is the first place they go to browse beauty products. Sephora has also made its retail presence a destination, with millennials and their friends turning Sephora shopping into a social occasion.[101]

Indulgence can be a powerful archetype if matched well to behaviors that align. Learning to express indulgence presents more opportunities to celebrate self, the senses and moments of pampering, in ways that heighten sensorial experiences and deepen emotional connections.

2-4

MODEL: STAGES

Similar to how people bond with each other, people bond with brands in a series of distinct stages. Stages reveal and measure the depth and degree of intensity of an intimate brand relationship. Together with archetypes, they form the foundation of the Brand Intimacy Model.

There are three core stages: sharing, bonding and fusing. Each stage builds on top of the other. In general, most brands have the majority of customers in the earliest stage of intimacy, sharing, and numbers generally drop as the stages grow in intensity. Like human relationships, positive experiences build stronger connections and deepen intimacy, while negative experiences pull the relationship down toward indifference.

Brand intimacy stages are unique for several reasons. First, they focus on reciprocity. Few other approaches highlight the idea of mutuality. What's important to take away across any of our three stages is that this is a relationship between two equals, like any good relationship on a personal level. This is no longer about traditional brand "push" or consumer "pull;" rather it suggests both are contributing and adding value. Second, these stages are more intense since they already involve being in a relationship. The stages are based on the fact that anyone who reaches the stage of sharing has already passed through earlier stages like awareness, consideration and preference. They are therefore more advanced and are associated with a powerful connection to a brand. We often say that brand intimacy is more of an elevated goal, one that is meant to measure, nurture, and enhance the bonds that exist.

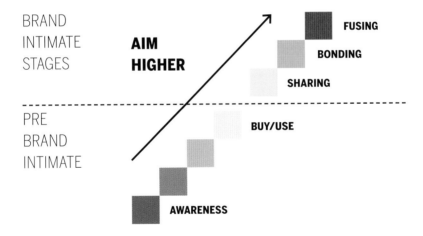

Through our work in correlating the degree of brand intimacy with financial performance (see the section on Value and Return), we have been able to demonstrate that the more customers are intimate with a brand, the better the business performance of the brand and the better the return on marketing investment. And the more intense the bonds are with your customers (e.g., fusing versus bonding or sharing), the better the performance yet again.

Brand intimacy stages help frame two ends of the marketing spectrum. At the outset, they help define the maturity of bonds a brand has with its stakeholders. Benchmark research can further detail the degree to which the brand is establishing emotional bonds and the relative percentage of those bonds by stage. Tracking movement across stages, as well as the overall percent of customers forming intimate relationships, is extremely valuable to remaining on top of one's public image and industry performance. At the opposite end of the spectrum, stages can inform how a brand goes to market. It can be an effective tool for aligning channels to those activities that are determined to build more sharing/bonding or fused stakeholders.

While there are distinct stages in brand intimacy, the "stages" referred to in our model are designed to make it easier to understand the process that consumers and brands go through. This comprises a number of emotional and rational milestones achieved when brand relationships become more intimate.

The real-life process, however, may not resemble the clear-cut, step-by-step progression depicted in our model. People might vacillate between two stages before moving forward; some stages, due to a variety of potential factors, might move faster or slower than others. A consumer might leave a brand relationship for a numbers of reasons, only to return with a stronger predisposition to the brand. The stages acknowledge and recognize the flexible and fluctuating nature of relationships. They are grounded in psychology and have been further corroborated by our quantitative research with consumers.

To better demostrate the role that stages play in forming intimate brands, we will illustrate the differences of each stage and how different brands manifest their performance.

Sharing

"I like when companies and customers participate together. This lets customers know they are important. IKEA is a good example."

German consumer

Bonding

"Nike is a brand I trust. I feel like they really understand me."

Japanese consumer

Fusing

"I love the Nabisco brand fully, and Nabisco loves me back by making me feel good with each bite I take! It returns its love to me through goodness of taste."

U.S. consumer

STAGES:

SHARING

SHARING OCCURS WHEN THE PERSON AND THE BRAND ENGAGE AND INTERACT. KNOWLEDGE IS BEING SHARED, AND THE PERSON IS INFORMED ABOUT WHAT THE BRAND IS ALL ABOUT (AND VICE VERSA). AT THIS STAGE, ATTRACTION OCCURS THROUGH RECIPROCITY AND ASSURANCE.

Disney is a brand my family and I connect with. My house is full of princesses and pageantry. My daughters identify with and are attracted to all things Disney.

Japanese consumer

VS.

Brand Example Demonstration:

NETFLIX

Netflix provides me with access to on demand entertainment. They get me. I get them.

U.S. consumer

SHARING

This is the earliest phase of brand intimacy, when a reciprocal relationship is established. There is knowledge being shared; the consumer is informed about what the brand is all about, and vice versa. At this stage, attraction occurs through reciprocity and assurance. Here, that sense of security mentioned by Erikson begins to be fostered (see Understanding Intimacy for more details on Erik Erickson's intimacy definition). Should the relationship advance, it would evolve to bonding, the next stage. Should it decline, it would likely cause disengagement fueled by indifference.

Disney and Netflix both engage consumers with entertainment—but from two opposite ends.

These two brands, both dominant forces in the entertainment industry, have a similar sharing performance despite wildly diverging business models. Disney is the iconic film, theme park, and global merchandise-churning behemoth, while Netflix is the young upstart video streaming service that perfectly typifies the digital disruption in entertainment delivery. Disney shows 47 percent of its users in some form of intimacy with the brand, while Netflix has 52 percent.

While these companies couldn't be more different, they are both building intimacy most dominantly through the sharing stage. Both brands take a different approach to gaining and remaining relevant—Disney, through its iconic characters, movies, and attractions, and Netflix through the ubiquity of devices and the ability to make personal the movie and TV show watching experience. Disney has the benefit of decades of brand building and a diversified portfolio that services families and their children from infancy through their teenage years; Netflix is the explosive upstart that is benefiting from the increasingly mobile and habit-forming behavior of its young users. Netflix ranked 25th overall in our 2015 study and rose to 5th position in 2017, moving up 19 spots. Now it is only two places behind Disney.

At present, however, the breadth of appeal for Disney's brand and its leadership in its category with a variety of users is stronger than Netflix. Disney's brand intimacy is fueled by the strong archetypes of nostalgia and identity—these are powerful assets for this iconic brand; a company that is synonymous with family entertainment and an emotionally powerful blend of magic and fun.

Netflix, the challenger, has instead built their brand intimacy around fulfillment and ritual. Their ability to deliver content and cater to the preferences of their users creates a very friction-free experience that further builds on the ritual of using the service. The ability to consume content at one's pace, especially in the form of binging (a behavior Netflix basically invented), creates a new world where time shrinks and the characters of the content become one's reality. Ask anyone who emerges from a binge session and you will hear how hard it can be to return to a normal routine—a form of detoxing or re-entering of society is often required.

Luke's Diner Pop-Up

An example of blurring real life and entertainment, Netflix celebrated the 16th anniversary of Gilmore Girls and its revival of the show on Netflix, by taking over 200 cafés and recreating the fictional café 'Luke's Diner' from Gilmore Girls.[102] Snapcodes were printed on 10,000 coffee cups that were distributed at the pop-up cafes for free. Once people took a picture of the Snapcode using the Snapchat app, they were prompted to apply the sponsored Gilmore Girls filter to their photos for one hour. The sponsored filter was viewed 880,000

HEAD TO HEAD

DISNEY	OVERALL RANK:	NETFLIX	OVERALL RANK:
Disney	**2**	NETFLIX	**5**
	INDUSTRY RANK:		INDUSTRY RANK:
	1		**2**

✦ ARCHETYPES

DISNEY

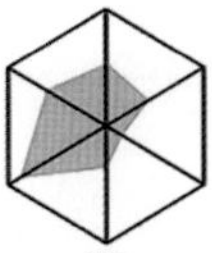

- FULFILLMENT 43
- INDULGENCE 50
- IDENTITY 35
- NOSTALGIA 72
- ENHANCEMENT 13
- RITUAL 29

NETFLIX

- FULFILLMENT 44
- INDULGENCE 43
- IDENTITY 21
- NOSTALGIA 14
- ENHANCEMENT 40
- RITUAL 50

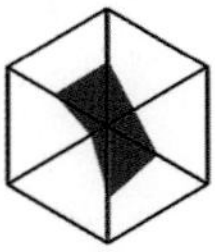

STAGES

DISNEY		NETFLIX	
FUSING	13%	FUSING	5%
BONDING	14%	BONDING	17%
SHARING	20%	SHARING	30%

QUOTIENT

DISNEY	NETFLIX
73.1	**61.2**

times. Snapchat reported that the one-day marketing event reached more than 500,000 people.[103] This one small example hints at how to engage and build a two-way relationship with consumers. Instead of asking consumers for something, Netflix created real Luke's Diners that people could visit and get free coffee and a mug from.[104] Fans got access to an exclusive filter (which could be activated only by taking a picture of the Snapcode). This, in turn, created wider reach for the brand because consumers shared their pictures.

Consumers respond to both Netflix and Disney by building relationships that seem to be strongest in sharing. This is the most common phase throughout all brands in our research. Disney, a mature and strong brand, also has a higher than average percentage of intimate customers in the ultimate stage of fusing; thus, by also increasing the funnel of new fans in sharing, Disney keeps itself strong with a broad range of customers in various stages of intimacy. It is successful at bringing in new audiences and parlaying those relationships into fusing.

Disney's Make-A-Wish

One example that demonstrates Disney's focus on sharing can be seen with its #ShareYourEars effort.To acknowledge the 100,000th Disney wish granted and the Disneyland resort's 60th anniversary, Disney teamed up with the Make-A-Wish Foundation and invited Disney fans to send images of themselves wearing Mickey Mouse Ears with the hashtag #ShareYourEars. For each shared photo, Disney pledged to donate $5 to the Make-A-Wish Foundation, with a limit of $1 million. Fans who donated $5 to the foundation were entered into a sweepstakes to win big prizes from Disney.

This campaign received overwhelming support and photo submissions. It highlights how to get customers to engage with the brand for a good cause, in this case by demonstrating consumer engagement with the iconic Disney ears, a form of intimacy in itself ("wearing" the brand). This effort also created a sense of shared values, pride and trust. Disney further enticed consumers with their sweepstakes and a chance to receive something special. Acknowledging the appeal, Disney also showed flexibility and consideration by doubling its donation.[105]

Like Disney, a preponderance of Netflix's users are in sharing. In fact, Netflix has more customers sharing than Disney. This suggests, as with Disney, that the brand has no shortage of users entering the intimacy funnel. Despite being a new brand, they have a broad range of appeal and are also above average in bonding. Netflix is at an average rate of fusing, suggesting more success in the first two phases of intimacy. Since Netflix has fewer customers in fusing, it will be interesting to see how this evolves over time. The brand's future looks promising, as binge watching is addictive, a quality that bodes well for leveraging the ritual archetype, a powerful intimacy driver.

Sharing is a key stage as it begins the formation of intimate feelings. This is a stage of great potential, where the relationship can prosper and grow. In this stage, consumers feel they can count on the brand to perform consistently, and often start to invest emotionally in the brand, making the relationship more of a two-way street.

In the last decade, Disney and Netflix have both invested heavily in areas that are capable of attracting new customers and strengthening bonds with existing ones. In 2012, Netflix began producing original content, and since then they've created countless successful TV shows and movies that are exclusively streamed on their service, which have won numerous awards. This dedication to content creation could be an attempt to create stronger bonds with their consumers, who now rely on the streaming service for more than just convenience. The exclusivity of the content is also likely to attract new subscribers who are eager to watch the new shows and movies that they can't stream anywhere else.

Disney has done some major investing of its own, most notably in the purchases of Marvel Entertainment in 2009 and Lucas Films in 2012. Spending roughly $4 billion on each of these companies, Disney now owns even more of the most iconic franchises in the world, including Star Wars and The Avengers. Like Netflix, they've invested in opportunities for new content, and because it's Disney, they've targeted two nostalgia gold mines. These acquisitions are probably intended to create new relationships rather than strengthen existing ones, but that doesn't mean stronger bonds aren't likely to form.

STAGES:

BONDING

BONDING IS WHEN AN ATTACHMENT IS CREATED, AND THE RELATIONSHIP BETWEEN A PERSON AND A BRAND BECOMES MORE SIGNIFICANT AND COMMITTED. THIS IS A STAGE OF ACCEPTANCE, AND TRUST IS ESTABLISHED.

BMW does a very good job creating intimate relationships with people...I have been purchasing BMWs since 1984, and I trust this brand.

U.S. consumer

VS.

Brand Example Demonstration:

Mercedes-Benz cars are engineered to help me escape convention, boredom and on occasion, gravity. It is a classic car, which has an important role in our life. Our relationship is established and I wouldn't try another car.

German consumer

The automotive industry produces the most intimate brand relationships, compared to fourteen other industries researched in our study. Cars and motorcycles are among the most significant purchases consumers make. The buying process and purchase decision are made only after great consideration and study to align with one's tastes, economic sensibilities and status/stage in life. It therefore shouldn't come as a surprise that almost one-third of the top 20 most intimate brands are cars or motorcycles.

These results suggest the strong bonds people have with their cars and the ability of this category to connect powerfully with consumers. Many archetypes score high in this industry for the top brands, as you would expect. Fulfillment of the brand (how well it exceeds expectations, delivers superior service, quality, and efficacy) remains a top deciding factor.

A nuance to understanding the importance of car brands related to fulfillment may be the safety factor. On the road, we need to be confident that our purchases are performing reliably and dependably. The necessity for car brands to be reliable can be especially important for the bonding stage, which involves building trust between the consumer and the brand. For consumers to truly bond with a brand, they need to know they can rely on their products, especially when it comes to their safety. Whether purchasing or leasing an automobile, the choice comes with a great deal of commitment. More than with other products, consumers will invest a great deal of money and time into their relationship with their car. This makes the bonding stage especially crucial for automotive brands. Perhaps that's why five of the top 20 brands with the highest rates of bonding are in the automotive space.

Another important aspect of automotive brand intimacy is the identity archetype. What a consumer chooses to drive speaks volumes about who they are, or, perhaps more importantly, how they see themselves. Especially with luxury brands, a car can be a clear indicator of lifestyle, status and personal values. Based on the price, size, speed, design, color, fuel-efficiency, special features, and country of origin of a car, a car can reflect a great deal about the person who owns it. In the bonding stage, acceptance and attachment are more significant, which may align well with those that identify a brand with identity.

The head to head chart contrasts a pair of similar automotive brands: BMW, the top-ranked automotive brand (#9 overall), and Mercedes (#56 overall). Both German luxury automakers are known for their quality and above-average performance across the brand intimacy archetypes of indulgence, fulfillment, and identity.

HEAD TO HEAD

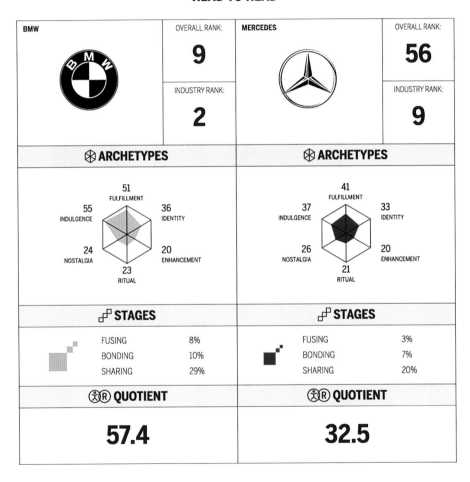

However, BMW has achieved a stronger brand intimacy quotient because more of its users have some form of intimacy with the brand (47 percent for BMW, compared to 30 percent for Mercedes), across all three stages. We can see where BMW has done a better job in connecting emotionally with its drivers and that translates to a much stronger, more intimate brand. Additionally, bonding scores increase among those 35 years and older and those making $75,000 or more.

BMW Ultimate Benefit Card

In this stage, where the relationship between consumer and brand becomes more committed and significant, one thing BMW does is reward series 7 customers with special incentives and offers as a way to offer more to build bonds. The Ultimate Benefits program encompasses lifestyle offerings, extending the relationship beyond the automotive realm.[106] BMW collaborates with premium brands to deliver luxurious experiences to their drivers. All BMW owners are entitled to these benefits, but BMW 7 series owners get access to an exclusive level of luxury services and personal attention. Benefits include access to prestigious sporting events, travel upgrades and priority restaurant reservations.[107]

In the meantime, has Mercedes lost its way? The brand has made committed strides after divesting itself of Chrysler and revamping its stodgy image and car design to better compete for younger buyers. Yet it still did not rank in the Top 100 Powerful Brands of 2016.[108] While sales and business seem to have improved, the brand itself does not seem to be innovating or advancing compared to years past. That said, Mercedes performs better with younger consumers than it does with older ones, although BMW still outperforms Mercedes across all ages. Older users (ages 35–64) prefer BMW, and Mercedes ranks higher among men than women. Car brands seem to perform best in the middle-income areas and with older adults. In extremes of income, the prevalence of intimate car brands diminishes. This suggests the brands maintain an overall appeal that requires the broadest demographic sample to maintain their ranking and stature.

Mercedes-Benz Club of America

A smart approach taken by Mercedes is the fostering of their Mercedes-Benz Club of America, or MBCA, a community of 30,000 people with a passion for Mercedes-Benz—those likely to be in the bonding stages.[109] Although it is not affiliated with Mercedes-Benz USA or Daimler-Benz AG, the club is sanctioned by MBUSA.[110] The community offers discussions and forums for every type of Mercedes user, from Women on Wheels and Young Guns to Gullwing, SLS and AMG.

It encourages people to get together to participate in rallies and test drive new car releases. The MBUSA group of technical advisors, drivers, restorers and engineers share their knowledge with other members on various topics related to the upkeep and maintenance of their Mercedes-Benz vehicles. This continues to deepen the connections, communications and brand experiences with other like-minded users.

While both brands try to connote trust, it's important to consider safety when reviewing stages for intimate car brands. Think of the major brand recalls or safety related issues that cars can have. From Toyota's incident seven years ago, to the more recent challenges faced by Volkswagen, safety issues and product recalls can have a major impact on consumers. Brand intimacy is hard to achieve and maintain. Like bonds between people, it requires sustained efforts and continual nurturing. Scandals and mishaps, especially those related to safety, can quickly erode trust and assurance exemplified in bonding.

While both Mercedes and BMW have intimate customers who are sharing, bonding, and fusing, it is notable that BMW is stronger across all the stages than Mercedes, and has more customers who are intimate.

We chose to compare these two brands because the intensity of the bonds they form are reflective of their products and their businesses—perennially enduring, solid, and rooted in excellence. The bonding stage reflects this level of intimacy clearly. Since sharing is the most popular phase and the initial stage of intimacy, and fusing is rarer and reflects a level of intimacy that smaller quantities of consumers reach, the bonding stage is effectively the pinnacle of brand intimacy for the largest number of consumers. BMW and Mercedes are both intimate brands with strong bonds, highlighting the ability of these brands to connect powerfully with customers.

As strong as automotive brands are in our study, we see that lately, many are partnering with highly specialized niche brands to distinguish themselves in a saturated and competitive luxury vehicle market. Top-end buyers particularly appreciate these partnerships, which seek to combine rareness and quality—when something's bespoke and not everybody knows about it. Yet niche brands are also appearing in mid-level luxury cars. Volvo contracted with Orrefors, the Swedish glassworks, to design a gear selector for its XC90 sport utility vehicle and its upcoming S90 sedan. The crystalline knob is etched with the studio's name, along with "Sweden"—a nod to the sort of national pride that automakers like to showcase. Compared with the cost of developing an all-new model, a shrewd relationship with a small brand can efficiently shift or reinforce consumer perceptions for a car maker or provide something more distinct and limited.[111]

With the dramatic evolution in this category caused by technology and with trends like car sharing and autonomous driving affecting every manufacturer, creating more intimate brands may be the underlying necessity for automotive brands in the long term. This is especially true for millennial consumers, who are more willing to use self-driving vehicles and car sharing services than older generations, and three times more likely to abandon their vehicles if costs increase or impacts to the environment are lessened.[112]

FUSING

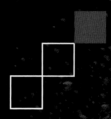

FUSING IS WHEN A PERSON AND A BRAND ARE INEXORABLY LINKED AND CO-IDENTIFIED. IN THIS STAGE, THE IDENTITIES OF THE PERSON AND THE BRAND BEGIN TO MERGE AND BECOME A FORM OF MUTUAL REALIZATION AND EXPRESSION.

Brand Example Demonstration:

Coca-Cola

Coca-Cola makes great quality products and have advertising and exposure that make me continue to buy their products on a regular basis. It is an essential part of my life.

U.S. consumer

VS.

Brand Example Demonstration:

Harley gives me a thrill—it is part of my identity. I love the freedom and rebel spirit inherent in the brand. I feel at one with the brand.

German consumer

The most desirable and powerful stage for a brand and consumer is the rare territory of fusing.

In the past, brands were eager to build loyalists—seemingly drone-like armies of passive servants obedient to the brand. As we know, the tables have turned; consumers today have more influence and impact regarding if a brand thrives or dies. However, many brands today have succeeded almost in spite of themselves. Think of the trapped loyalty that some brands have benefited from—consumers who regularly use products because they either cannot change or feel unable to justify the pain of switching. The utility companies, telecommunications, cable companies and other former monopolistic entities are typical brands with these trapped stakeholders.

So, if loyalty isn't the best place to aim a brand's performance, then where should it be aimed?

Fusing is the ultimate stage in an intimate relationship, where the brand is an extension of a person's personality and values. Fusing is when a consumer and a brand are inexorably linked and co-identified. This is a very powerful stage and very significant in terms of the potential for what a brand and a person can experience. Harley Davidson is a brand with among the highest rates of fusing. Its success in building intimacy is based on the fact that its product is more than a motorcycle; it's a lifestyle, one centered on emotional attachment and pride. This is true whether you're an employee or a buyer, or both. Customers not only buy the product and its merchandise, they tattoo the brand's logo on their body, they attend rallies and company sponsored events. Leveraging the powerful connection people feel to Harley, the company created The Harley Owners Group, an organization that sponsors rallies, offers special promotions and keeps Harley owners in close contact with the company and each other. Today, this group has more than 365,000 members in 940 chapters throughout the world.[113] It contributes to charities the group admires, and enables both members and the brand to create a community of shared interests and activities. Harley has also started to do more traditional advertising and social efforts to broaden their audience; however, its core success has been in its ability to translate emotional attachment into a powerful community of devotees through events and merchandise.

Harley Davidson Owners Group

In brand intimacy, we focus on the bonds that form between brands and consumers, and believe that all three stages of brand intimacy are more reciprocal
and rewarding territories for brands and their users. When you become two
halves of the same coin, you're fusing—a blurred and blissful state of co-
identification. In this powerful stage, the brand and the user are almost one and
the same in terms of values, tastes, and expression. Consumers, employees,
and stakeholders of fused brands are their biggest evangelists. Brands here
embody the needs and desires of their most ardent users. The result is a
synergistic, mutually beneficial, and unshakable bond. We believe being fused
is a better form of loyalty, a new and more desirable end state for a brand.

Diet Coke Campaign

Another example is Diet Coke, who celebrated their biggest fans by selecting
over 50 fan tweets and turned them into beautiful visual representations in the
real world. Partnering with illustrators, painters, sculptors, and graphic artists,
Diet Coke created magazine ads, cakes, billboards, clothes, jewelry, and more,
all using the adoring tweets of their biggest fans. After years of connecting with

their most passionate fans through social media, Diet Coke felt they needed to return their appreciation in a big, real way, again creating reciprocity and a feeling of being co-identified.[114, 115]

Coca-Cola and Harley-Davidson are two brands that demonstrate the benefits of fusing. Both are iconic and quintessential brands that have thrived for decades, with a powerful and devoted following. These brands both embody emotional connection and the rewards of connecting deeply with consumers.

HEAD TO HEAD

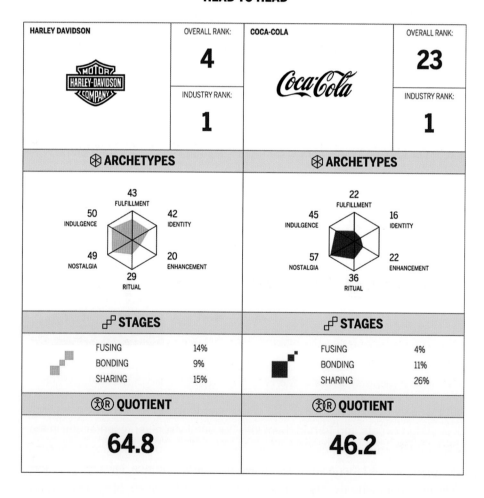

HARLEY DAVIDSON		COCA-COLA	
	OVERALL RANK: **4**		**OVERALL RANK:** **23**
	INDUSTRY RANK: **1**		**INDUSTRY RANK:** **1**

⊛ ARCHETYPES	⊛ ARCHETYPES
FULFILLMENT 43 INDULGENCE 50 — IDENTITY 42 NOSTALGIA 49 — ENHANCEMENT 20 RITUAL 29	FULFILLMENT 22 INDULGENCE 45 — IDENTITY 16 NOSTALGIA 57 — ENHANCEMENT 22 RITUAL 36

⊡ STAGES		⊡ STAGES	
FUSING	14%	FUSING	4%
BONDING	9%	BONDING	11%
SHARING	15%	SHARING	26%

⊗ QUOTIENT	⊗ QUOTIENT
64.8	**46.2**

Coca-Cola, which ranked 23rd overall in our study and has a quotient score of 46.2, has two times its industry average of fused consumers, a testament to the bonds formed over generations and the status of the brand.

Even more impressive is how the bonds they've formed seem to be mainly around the combination of nostalgia and ritual—two deeply emotional and rooted archetypes that drive behavior. For those that remember the powerful advertising of Coca-Cola through decades, from the "I'd like to buy the world a Coke" display of diversity to the touching Mean Joe Greene ad, this brand has tried to become synonymous with American culture and a simple way to enjoy the moment.

Further highlighting its strength, Coca-Cola performs equally well with men and women and ranks consistently across income brackets. The only slightly concerning sign for Coca Cola is that is performs more strongly with older versus younger consumers, suggesting it may need to find more ways to engage millennials. When asked about being willing to pay 20 percent more for Coca Cola products, 17 percent of our total users agreed, 6 percent more price resilience than the category average.

As we expected, Harley-Davidson tops all automotive brands and ranks second overall in terms of fused customers at 14 percent—more than double the industry average in the automotive category (which, as we mentioned, contains one third of the top ten most intimate brands). This is a profound performance by a brand that is emotionally charged and forms strong bonds with consumers.

It shouldn't come as a surprise that the intimacy stage associated with co-identification is where Harley-Davidson thrives. Their iconic bikes are an integral part of their riders' lifestyle, and the brand name is aesthetically synonymous with leather jackets, bandanas, and handlebar mustaches. Their customers don't just love the brand; they become the brand, engulfed in its quintessential look and surrounded by other like-minded riders. Harley riders are perhaps more willing than any other customer to merge with their brand.

Few brands in our rankings perform as well across all the archetypes as Harley-Davidson. Only one archetype out of the six failed to score high for the brand—enhancement—and that is because it is less relevant for Harley users. This creates a profound mix of supercharged archetypes that combine to propel this brand and the bonds it creates forward.

Harley ranks strongest with men. It also ranks highest among those 35 years old and older, and performs well across all income levels. Regarding economic equity, among its fusing customers, 18 percent were willing to pay 20 percent more for Harley-Davidson products. Like Coca-Cola, Harley's stronger performance with older consumers could potentially hurt them in the long run, as millennials are now the largest demographic in the United States.

However, Harley seems up to the challenge. They've recently released bikes aimed toward this younger demographic, including an electric prototype, Project LiveWire. These bikes are cheaper, smaller, and more stripped-down than traditional Harleys, because the company understands that this generation is different, valuing simplicity and design over status and flash.[116]

Harley has also attempted to expand their base with the "Roll Your Own" campaign, which celebrates individuality while challenging the stereotype of the typical Harley rider. Their recent focus on foreign sales has also been represented in their brand. For example, Brazilian Harley dealers serve pastries and espresso to their customers on Saturday morning, building a sense of community and showing their customers acceptance and respect.[117] These additions to the Harley brand represent an invitation to new riders that builds on the loyal base of millions of baby boomers.

2-5

MODEL: BRAND INTIMACY QUOTIENT

The model culminates in a Brand Intimacy Quotient, established through our quantitative research. This is a score each brand receives indicating its performance. The Quotient is a composite measure that reflects the intensity of the relationship between consumers and brands as well as the prevalence (usage) of the brand. The higher the Quotient score, the more intense the emotional relationship with a brand. This makes it easy to compare, contrast and review results between competitors, as well as performance from previous years.

The Quotient is a score out of 100 assigned to any brand that is part of our brand intimacy research. The score is based on the amount of intimate users a brand has, as well as the type of intimate relationships consumers have with the brand (e.g., sharing, bonding or fusing). Based on a brand's performance against the six archetypes, each brand is assigned an "intensity of relationship" score. This score is a composite measure that takes into account the percentage of consumers at each stage of intimacy (indifference, sharing, bonding, fusing). Based on the Structural Equation Model, weights are assigned to each stage of intimacy, with fusing receiving the greatest weight on the overall intensity of relationship score, and indifference receiving the smallest weight.

It is important to note that the Quotient provides more than a ranking of brand performance and was specifically designed to provide prescriptive guidance to marketers. We modeled data to quantify the mechanisms that drive intimacy, resulting in a guide that allows marketers to better understand which dimensions need to be leveraged to build intimacy between their brand and consumers.

WHY OUR MODEL IS DISTINCT

Our model was created based on the way people behave and build relationships. We've applied what we've learned from advances in neuroscience, psychology, and behavioral science to create an approach designed to be realistic and reflective of the way people process information and make decisions. Our model is not an artificial marketing construct or contrived behavioral spectrum. It is based on representative stages that people pass through in order to achieve intimacy with a product or service.

Brand intimacy results in meaningful and reciprocal relationships that create more business growth, greater profit and higher pricing permissions. It requires companies to look at brand management from a holistic perspective. Everything a company does, including how it does things, makes a difference. Everything matters; everything moves the relationship between customer and brand closer or contributes, even in small ways, to its eventual end. Beyond pure marketing functions, this relates to product performance, IT, customer service, and operations. This approach also necessitates a thorough examination of how all stakeholders of the brand can impact and influence outcomes.

The model is mutual, based on reciprocity. This is important because it involves the interaction between a person and a brand at each stage of the engagement. We don't just look at how a person is behaving; we look at how a brand is performing. This gives us opportunity to provide brands with recommendations

BRAND INTIMACY MODEL

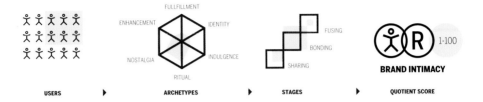

| USERS | ▶ | ARCHETYPES | ▶ | STAGES | ▶ | QUOTIENT SCORE |

on what they can do to improve their intimacy levels. Intimacy is, after all, an evolved state; it's not something you initially arrive at, it's a condition that needs to be fostered and nurtured. Other models may state that a brand has an awareness or consideration issue; however, it usually does not answer "why?" Our focus on the condition of intimacy constantly reimagines and re-dimensions relationships between people and brands in more significant ways.

Clearly, the pull of intimacy and indifference in our model is unique relative to most other branding constructs. It seems obvious and simple, yet no other model really acknowledges the fact that at any stage in brand building— something negative can happen, and if it does, the customer is at risk. We as brand builders have to understand that we can work to prevent these falls, and barring that, we can mitigate the damage and work to rebuild the relationship.

The model gives us the ability to create a unique set of rankings that assess the emotional connections between consumers and brands. We can understand which industries have the greatest propensity toward intimacy and which are more challenged; consider gender, age and income implications; and as you have already seen, comparisons between competitors or similarly performing brands. These rich insights can provide new perspectives on established brands and help decode disruptors and upstarts alike.

2-6

MODEL: RANKINGS

BRAND INTIMACY

3 ▀▀ ▐▮▌ ▐▬
GEOGRAPHIES

15
INDUSTRIES

400
BRANDS

12,000
CONSUMERS

100,000
BRAND EVALUATIONS

In our search to better understand brand intimacy—how it works, how it doesn't work, and how it can be cultivated—our best tool is insights. Our quantitative research, which represents, to our knowledge, the most comprehensive rankings of brands based on emotion to date, helped shape and validate our entire approach. Our goal was to benchmark how emotions impact brand relationships, and further dimension which brands are most successful at creating these bonds. This high-level introduction to the rankings reveals which industries and brands are succeeding in building strong bonds with customers.

It also starts to identify best performers and highlights nuances based on age, gender and income. While we know brand intimacy occurs across all segments, it is valuable to clarify distinctions and better understand the way building bonds is impacted by a variety of forces.

Our ranking of the Top 10 Most Intimate Ranked Brands highlights the strongest performing intimate brands.

U.S. TOP 10 MOST INTIMATE BRANDS 2017

RANK	BRANDS	⊗Ⓡ QUOTIENT
#1	(Apple)	↑ 77.0
↑ #2	Disney	↑ 73.1
↑ #3	amazon	↑ 71.0
↑ #4	HARLEY-DAVIDSON	↑ 64.8
↑ #5	NETFLIX	↑ 61.2
↑ #6	Nintendo	↑ 59.6
↑ #7	SAMSUNG	59.0
#8	WHOLE FOODS	↓ 58.8
↓ #9	BMW	↓ 57.4
↓ #10	TOYOTA	↓ 56.6

Arrows in green depict an improved performance vs. 2015 scores.
Arrows in red show a declining performance vs. 2015.

Among our Top 10, Apple takes first place, as it does in most surveys. Apple is a dominant force in the technology sector; interestingly, Samsung, in 7th place, is the only other technology brand to make this list. Three of the other brands are in the automotive industry, highlighting this category's high potential for creating intimacy between its brands and consumers. In addition, two very different retail brands make our list: Amazon, an online marketplace that promises a wide breadth of offerings; and its new acquisition, Whole Foods, a more upscale brick-and-mortar supermarket catering to those seeking fresh foods. We also see two distinct entertainment brands ranking: Disney, the entertainment conglomerate known for a focus on audiences, and Netflix, the streaming innovator, round out the Top 10.

As you can see, the highest ranked brand, Apple, has a quotient score of 77. This may seem on the low side, especially when reviewing the entire top 10 list and noting that Toyota, for example, ranks 10th with a quotient score of 56.6. We believe this is because brand intimacy is a new approach, one that marketers have not been consciously trying to build on. Additionally, as we've mentioned, not every consumer has intimate relationships with every brand they use; in fact, it's likely very few do at present, so we don't imagine brands are likely to score 100 prior to implementing directed changes to their marketing strategy.

INDUSTRIES

Among the fifteen industries we surveyed, automotive is the strongest performing, with an average Brand Intimacy Quotient of 44.5 (the average across all of our fifteen categories is 28.7). Given the close relationship people have with their cars and motorcycles, as well as the aspirational nature of this industry, this is to be expected. Media and entertainment had a strong showing in second place, highlighting the need consumers have for comfort and distraction these days. Retail came in third, with a particularly strong performance from Amazon. Technology and telecommunications was fourth, again showcasing the important role these brands play in our lives. Insurance and investing scored on the lower side. More surprising, luxury ranked 14th out of 15 categories, suggesting premium brands are not doing as much as expected to build emotional connections. Travel was the poorest performing category, garnering an industry average quotient of 14.7. Perhaps the increasing complexity of travel and commoditized promotions has limited its appeal for U.S. consumers, but regardless, this does show us that certain industries may find it more challenging to develop intimate relationships with their customers.

AVERAGE BRAND INTIMACY QUOTIENT SCORES BY INDUSTRY

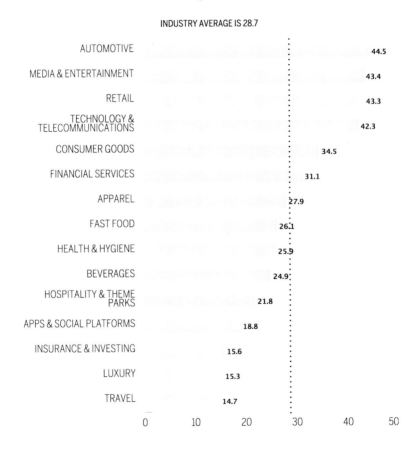

INDUSTRY AVERAGE IS 28.7

Industry	Score
AUTOMOTIVE	44.5
MEDIA & ENTERTAINMENT	43.4
RETAIL	43.3
TECHNOLOGY & TELECOMMUNICATIONS	42.3
CONSUMER GOODS	34.5
FINANCIAL SERVICES	31.1
APPAREL	27.9
FAST FOOD	26.1
HEALTH & HYGIENE	25.9
BEVERAGES	24.9
HOSPITALITY & THEME PARKS	21.8
APPS & SOCIAL PLATFORMS	18.8
INSURANCE & INVESTING	15.6
LUXURY	15.3
TRAVEL	14.7

Although some brands are strong across many archetypes and stages, we did find some unique focused examples. For example, a brand may "own" a specific archetype in the hearts and minds of consumers, or it may be notable for its degree of sharing, bonding, or fusing customers. The following reveals some interesting examples of brand intimacy.

(Apple logo)	Apple is our top-ranked brand overall. It is also the highest rated across several considerations, helping explain its dominance. For archetypes, Apple scored highest for enhancement (just edging out Google), ritual and identity. Apple also ranks #1 for "can't live without," meaning it would be very difficult to live without this brand. It also ranks highest for frequency of use (where Facebook also took 2nd place).
Disney	Disney, our #2 ranked brand, ranked highest for the archetype of nostalgia, which focuses on memories of the past and the warm, poignant feelings associated with them.
TOYOTA	Our #10 brand, Toyota, came in 1st for fulfillment, as it did in our 2015 study. This is linked with exceeding expectations, service, quality and efficacy.
HERSHEY'S	Hershey is seen as the most indulgent brand, centered on moments of pampering and gratification.
(Apple logo) NETFLIX (Nintendo)	Apple has the largest percentage of fusing customers, topping Harley-Davidson, which was #1 in our previous study. Netflix has the largest percentage of bonding customers, whereas Nintendo has the largest percentage of sharing customers.
NETFLIX	Netflix is the new Amazon. This year's performance indicates Netflix has risen as a top intimate brand and is becoming a significant force.
(Apple logo) amazon	Interestingly, both Amazon and Apple are more successful than most companies at crossing age groups and income levels.
SAMSUNG	Samsung is seen as the "poor man's" Apple by some, as it ranks #2 among those making $35-49,999.

WHAT DOES THIS TELL US?

DEMOGRAPHICS

When viewing intimate brands by age, you can see a range of insights. Apple and Amazon are both listed across all ages, highlighting their relevance from millennials to older adults. Netflix is only listed by those 18–34, Target by those 35–44 and Harley Davidson and Whole Foods by those 45–64, showcasing some specific preferences by age. Media and entertainment makes up half the list for those 18–34 years old, while retail comprises 50 percent of the top four brands among those 35–44 and 45–64 years old. Interestingly those 18–34 years old and those 35–44 years old have very similar lists, with three of the same four brands (Apple, Amazon and Disney), albeit in different orders.

AGE SNAPSHOTS

RANK	18-34	35-44	45-54
#1	Disney	Apple	Apple
#2	amazon	amazon	amazon
#3	NETFLIX	Harley Davidson	Harley Davidson
#4	Apple	Disney	Disney

What's notable here is that consumers below age 35 show more propensity to develop intimate relationships with brands, and appear more open to exploring those relationships, with a higher percentage in sharing. Overall, however, rates of bonding and fusing are essentially the same, suggesting age does not impact one's ability to form and maintain intimate relationships with brands.

STAGES OF INTIMACY BY AGE

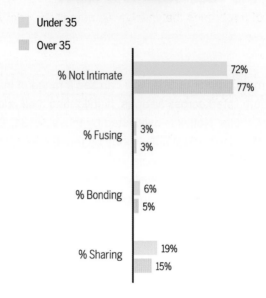

Under 35
Over 35

% Not Intimate — 72% / 77%

% Fusing — 3% / 3%

% Bonding — 6% / 5%

% Sharing — 19% / 15%

GENDER

Gender also provides interesting insights. Although men and women are similar in their overall level of intimacy with brands, the brands they identify with can be different. In general, women connect with a broad and more mature stable of brands than men do, preferring brands that are practical or relevant to their lifestyles.

GENDER BRAND LANDSCAPE

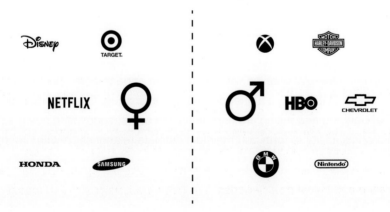

From observing the top five brands for women, we see that women have an interesting range of top brands that involve aspects of their daily life. Their top five brands include two entertainment and two retail brands. For men, two of their five top brands are automotive. While women listed Disney and Netflix for entertainment, men ranked Nintendo. Both genders had Amazon and Apple on their top five lists. A Nielsen study found that women's most trusted brands relate to convenience or their households, while trusted brands for men included more indulgent options (which seems to echo the Brand Intimacy findings to some degree.)[118]

TOP BRANDS BY GENDER

Top 5 Brands for Women	Top 5 Brands for Men
Disney	Apple
Apple	Harley-Davidson
amazon	Nintendo
Target	Chevrolet
NETFLIX	amazon

Overall, men and women are quite similar in the archetypes they ascribe to intimate brands, but there are a few nuances. Ritual, which is when a brand is ingrained into daily actions and is an important part of someone's daily life, plays a bigger role with women for brands in the financial services, retail, consumer goods, health and hygiene, social media and apps, fast food, and insurance and investing categories. In other words, using a brand repeatedly so that it becomes essential is a more significant indicator of intimacy for women than for men. This also aligns with the study, "Decoding the Female Consumer & Brand Loyalty," which observed that brands with a clear and relevant purpose that aligned with women's personal interests and values sometimes outranked brands that spend more on marketing.[119] Not everything is completely practical, however; indulgence, the archetype centering on pampering and gratification, is stronger among women overall.

When you compare women 18–34 with men of the same age, you see an even bigger distinction. Retail and entertainment (Disney and Netflix) is dominant with younger women, yet with men of the same age, entertainment (specifically gaming) dominates (with automotive remaining the other category of significance). Automotive brands are completely absent from women here. As mentioned earlier, women also lead with more practical, daily brands—brands that they count on for communication (Apple), ease of shopping (Amazon), every day purchases (Target), and to escape and unwind (like Disney/Netflix). Men are largely focused on gaming brands, which may also be for escape and comfort, although a different subset of entertainment.

TOP 5 BRANDS WOMEN VS. MEN

Women 18-34	Men 18-34
Disney	Nintendo
Apple	PlayStation
amazon	Xbox
NETFLIX	Harley-Davidson
Target	BMW

INCOME

Based on our findings, what role does income play in brand intimacy and consumer affection? As income increases, so too does the likelihood of having emotional relationships in automotive, technology and telecommunications, and retail.

We found quite a few differences when looking at intimate brands by income. Only Amazon was in the top 5 (interestingly in third place for both) among those making $35,000–50,000 as well as those earning $100,000–150,000. However, entertainment brands secured the #1 spot for both groups and technology the #2 spot, retail the #3. While the categories may be similar in many cases, the brands themselves are different. Apple is the technology brand of choice for the higher income group, while Samsung performs better with those making $35,000–50,000. PlayStation also ranks highest with this group, and Netflix is among their top brands, while Disney is preferred among the $100,000–150,000 group. Here, automotive brand Ford ranks in the top five as well.

INCOME SNAPSHOTS

RANK	35K-49K	75K-100K
#1	Disney	Apple
#2	Apple	amazon
#3	amazon	Disney
#4	NETFLIX	WHOLE FOODS
#5	Harley-Davidson	Toyota

IMPLICATIONS

Based on extensive consumer research, the Brand Intimacy Model features four core components: the user with a strong emotional connection, archetypes, stages and a brand intimacy quotient.

Successful intimate brands leverage up to six brand archetypes to create strong connections.

Brand intimacy stages determine the intensity of brand-consumer relationships. The higher the stage, the greater the return (or performance).

Top ranked intimate brands provide insights on who's doing it well and why. Seeing brands ranked by age, gender and income further details the way distinct demographics build bonds.

3

METHODS & PRACTICE

From the financial strength of intimate brands to guarding against their pitfalls, here we showcase our approach for building intimate brands and our future focus on software that helps manage and enable intimacy through collaboration, simulators and real-time tracking of emotions.

3-1

VALUE AND RETURN

Could brands that have stronger bonds with their customers correlate to better business performance? The answer is definitively, yes.

Increasingly, companies are looking for new ways to grow. Over the past decade we've seen that supply chains and operations have been optimized and made extremely lean. Growth via acquisition comes with its own complexities and challenges, and growth via innovation and new product development can feel like trying to catch lightning in a bottle. At the same time, executives and shareholders are overlooking ways to leverage their brand and its vast potential.

We believe brands designed for today's complexity have the capacity to cultivate emotional bonds with customers. We now know those bonds create **a major business benefit to being an intimate brand.**

We uncovered the value of intimate brands by first compiling published financial data from the Top 10 companies in the Brand Intimacy Rankings, the Standard & Poor's 500 and the Fortune 500. For each brand, our teams gathered the reported revenue and profit/loss for the years 2005–2015 from their annual reports and/or Form 10-Ks. Our goal was to assess which brands performed best in revenue and profit annually and also over a duration of time.

Here is the summary of what we found:

GREATER LONGEVITY

Intimate brands excel over time, creating tremendous value and demonstrating performance longevity. Over the last 10 years, the revenue from top intimate brands nearly doubles the S&P and nearly triples Fortune 500.

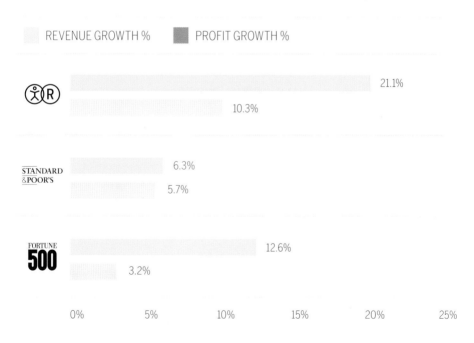

BRAND GROWTH & LONGEVITY FROM 2005 TO 2015

REVENUE GROWTH %   PROFIT GROWTH %

21.1%
10.3%

STANDARD &POOR'S
6.3%
5.7%

FORTUNE 500
12.6%
3.2%

0%   5%   10%   15%   20%   25%

Keep in mind these percentage differences for larger companies translates to massive dollar amounts. Using Apple as an example, even the slimmest profit advantage of 1 percent can generate an additional $843 million swing (based on 2016 quarterly earnings.)[120]

From this data, the average year-over-year growth rates for both revenue and profit over a 10-year period were calculated.

MORE GROWTH

We next wanted to better quantify the advantages represented by revenue and profit into annual dollar figures, which would in turn make them easier to evaluate, compare and contrast at a glance.

In order to determine the total dollar value of brand growth, we compounded the total revenue and profit for our Top 10 Most Intimate Brands by applying each of our calculated average year-over-year growth rates from the respective indices. We then compared this figure to the calculated total dollar value of growth for Standard & Poor's 500 and Fortune 500, and took the average.

AVG. ANNUAL PROFIT

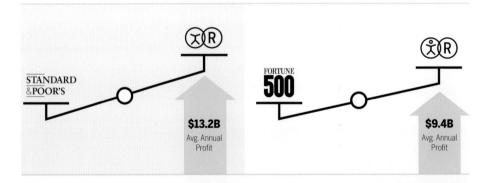

What did our calculations reveal? Turns out, on an *annual basis,* top intimate ranked brands are adding $13.2 billion *more* profit than S&P companies. Compared to the Fortune 500 companies, intimate brands add $9.4 billion in annual profit. These are profound advantages and clearly demonstrate the business performance advantage of intimate brands.

HIGHER PRICE RESILIENCE

Another important area where more intimate brands outperform is on price. As consumers move up from non-intimacy to the highest stage of intimacy (fusing), their willingness to pay a premium for a brand increases. In other words, there is a strong correlation between economic equity and the levels of intimacy with a brand. You can see in our chart that, among those consumers who are not intimate with a brand, an average of 4 percent were willing to pay 20 percent more for its products, services or offerings. This steadily increases as a consumer progresses across the stages of intimacy, from sharing, to bonding, to fusing. In sharing the percentage doubles, from 4 percent to 8 percent (on average). Let's use Apple as an example. Apple has over 700 million iPhone users worldwide.[121] For the purposes of this example, let's assume they are all in the sharing stage. That means that Apple has more than 56 million users willing to pay 20 percent more for their phones.

As consumers move up the stages of intimacy, we see even more startling advantages for brands regarding price performance. In the category of bonding (where the relationship between a person and a brand becomes more signifi-cant and committed), 14 percent of consumers indicated that they were willing to pay 20 percent more for their intimate brands—that's more than three times the number of non-intimate consumers willing to pay more. Finally, with people who have fused with the brand (when a person and a brand are inexorably linked and co-identified), the advantage is 21 percent are willing to pay more, or more than 5 times those that aren't intimate with the brand. For Apple, to use the example again, with 700 million fused iPhone users, this would translate to more than 147 million of them willing to pay 20 percent more. Though these numbers are extrapolated for effect, it is easy to see how Apple continues to outperform its competitors on margin—the quality of their products combined with the power of its brand to deliver exceptional brand intimacy.

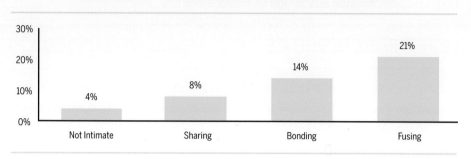

PERCENTAGE OF CONSUMERS WILLING TO PAY 20% MORE

To further visualize this advantage, we took the average percentage of fused consumers willing to pay 20 percent more for all brands in our study and compared it to the best-performing brand with respect to price resilience, Amazon. We found that 30 percent of Amazon fused users have a willingness to pay a 20 percent premium for their brand. That is approaching almost one-third of their most intimate users, each willing to pay a premium.

COMMANDING PRICE PREMIUMS AMONG FUSED USERS

Another example is viewing the Top 10 Intimate Brands versus the bottom 10 ranking brands in terms of economic equity. We found the Top 10 brands are 50 percent more likely to command a premium and are three times more likely to pay 20 percent more over the bottom 10 brands.

TOP BRANDS OUTPERFORM

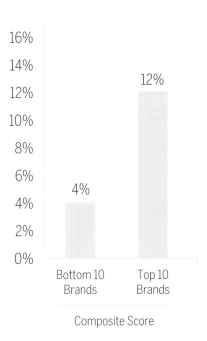

When we continued to explore the role of intimacy on price performance, we found that brands with higher brand intimacy quotient scores correlate to having stronger economic equity profiles. In other words, the stronger the intimacy, the more willing consumers are to purchase and pay more. To dimension this point, we chose two brands within one category which are typically competitors. For each pair, Delta and American, and Chrysler and Honda, the brand with the higher quotient outperforms its competitor in consumer willingness to pay more.

PERCENTAGE WILLINGESS TO PURCHASE

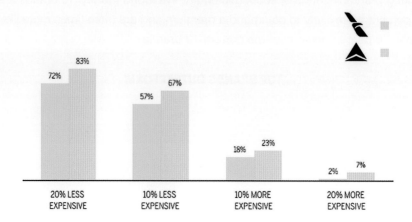

	20% LESS EXPENSIVE	10% LESS EXPENSIVE	10% MORE EXPENSIVE	20% MORE EXPENSIVE
	72% / 83%	57% / 67%	18% / 23%	2% / 7%

PERCENTAGE WILLINGESS TO PURCHASE

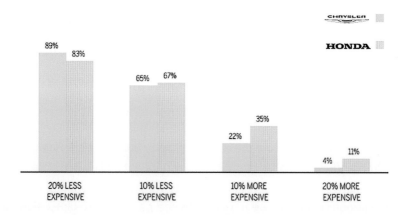

CHRYSLER
HONDA

	20% LESS EXPENSIVE	10% LESS EXPENSIVE	10% MORE EXPENSIVE	20% MORE EXPENSIVE
	89% / 83%	65% / 67%	22% / 35%	4% / 11%

Even in two disparate industries, such as airlines and automotive (which are the highest and lowest ranked industries, respectively), the more intimate the brand, the better the price performance.

From assessing the data, it also became clear that consumers are willing to pay more for certain industries over others. The top five industries with the largest number of consumers willing to pay more are: consumer goods, media and entertainment, fast food, technology and telecommunications, and beverages. In general, these involve the purchase of lower priced items, which may make people less sensitive about potentially paying more as well as being frequently used products and services. However, media and entertainment and technology and telecommunications are two industries where offerings could be costly and they still rank high for price resilience.

What is most important to highlight is the higher the intimacy performance, the more price resilience a brand has.

3-2

FAILURES, PERSPECTIVES AND LESSONS

Brands today are under tremendous pressure to differentiate, perform, and deliver. There are more channels and greater expectations than ever before for new content, fresh ideas, customized offers, and frequent (but not overbearing) communications. Many marketers hope that continuing their same-old, same-old will suffice; however, there are too many examples of consumers using social media and other forums to vent about brands being uncommunicative, lazy, or out of date to believe that what worked yesterday will continue to work today. Simply put, consumers now have different expectations of brands—expecting them to be smarter, relevant, trustworthy, and quick acting.

Having written about theory, we wanted to provide some tangible examples, so we've included some painful brand experiences that demonstrate missteps, which have helped move customers from intimate to indifferent. These should serve as warnings to us all; while mistakes are inevitable, there are ways to avoid common pitfalls or activities that are clearly oriented toward destroying consumer bonds.

WHEN BRANDS FAIL: AVOIDING THE PITFALLS OF INDIFFERENCE

Since emotion is the fuel of brand intimacy, the upside of being bonded with a brand is powerful. The downside, however, is dire. As with human relationships, brands and people form equally complex and emotionally driven connections. We can all relate to horrible breakups, where once-loving relationships become minefields. The same holds true for brands. As we began to understand why people choose, love, or are loyal to brands, we became equally intrigued as to why and how they become frustrated, hateful, or enraged toward them. How does this happen? And how does it eventually lead to indifference?

We've found that the causes of consumer indifference are an area of little collective study—and who wants to dwell on the negative, after all? It's easy to be overwhelmed by the many published lists of "top" brands, yet finding any organized "worst of" study proves difficult. All the same, we believe learning from the lessons of brand failures is difficult, albeit critically important.

At the risk of dwelling on schadenfreude, brands today face increasingly new and severe risks. Today, companies looking to optimize and maximize their bottom-line performance are trying to do more with fewer resources. At the same time, consumers feel increasingly empowered through a wealth of choices and a realization of the impact they can leverage over brands. Anger and indifference, when enabled by the viral and compounding effects of the social web, can make any marketing executive feel like he or she is fighting a losing battle.

Beyond the risk to reputation and the performance of a brand, we have discovered that consumers can reach a more potent and permanent state of ambivalence. Think of it as worse than hatred—devoid of emotional connection of any kind, and worst of all, likely irreversible. We've collected a series of examples that illustrate how consumer bonds with brands can be abused or, in some cases, destroyed.

COMCAST AND THE SOUND OF INDIFFERENCE

In this cringe-inducing call, a customer is antagonized and tortured through a separation process that one must hear to believe. The customer is trying to cancel their service, and repeatedly makes this request clearly. They note that they do not owe any explanation to Comcast as to why they want to discontinue usage and are simply requesting a cancellation. The customer service agent, in response, is unbearable, suggesting that the customer has to convince him as to why cancellation is necessary. He repeatedly requests information on what Comcast has done wrong, why the customer is dissatis-fied, and what service he plans to use next. Amazingly, the caller remains calm throughout and holds his ground (likely because he knew it would make for better theater later). Here is a short snippet:

> Rep: I'm just trying to figure out what it is about Comcast service that you don't want to keep.

> Customer: This phone call is actually a really amazing representative example of why I don't want to stay with Comcast.

> Customer: The way you can help me is by disconnecting my service.

> Rep: But how is that helping you! How is that helping you? Explain to me how that is helping you!

> Rep: OK, but I'm trying to help you!

The indifference in the customer's voice demonstrates that he is past the point of having any feelings about this brand. It also makes it clear there is little the Comcast brand could ever to do rebuild this relationship. This story made a big splash in social channels and has prompted additional embarrassing findings for Comcast, such as the training manual that essentially prescribes the behavior on this call. To hear the conversation visit mblm.com/brandintimacybook.

Comcast and the Sound of Indifference

IMPACT

Customers who consider that they are trapped by the brands they use are prone to slipping into a state of complete indifference. They believe their ability to choose has been removed. Utility brands or government brands are common culprits. Companies such as Comcast must find ways for their customers (especially if a significant subset of repeat customers perceive they are stuck) to avoid feeling like prisoners. In fact, it's worth stressing that where there is a potential for customers to feel trapped, or believe they have no say in the relationship, extra caution should be taken.

LESSON LEARNED: RECOGNIZE WHEN A CUSTOMER IS A PRISONER TO YOUR BRAND AND MITIGATE RISKS.

UNITED BREAKS GUITARS/
PASSENGER DRAGGED OFF PLANE

Dave Carroll, playing his (unbroken) guitar

This piece of viral gold is now over nine years old! A United Airlines traveler was so upset that his guitar was broken on a flight that he created a song and music video. Over 2.4 million people have viewed this compelling and humorous takedown of a brand that created indifference by acting indifferent. The traveler details his experience, including dealing with disinterested United staff who gave him the runaround for months, a variety of phone numbers and follow ups that went nowhere and the frustration of feeling invisible. This social media marketing classic is also a book and case study: visit mblm.com/brandintimacybook to see more about this incident.

More recently, United found itself back on the hot seat, facing a backlash by having police forcibly remove a ticketed customer off a plane. The event was recorded by fellow passengers and played across virtually every news program, inducing outrage. The situation was further exacerbated by United's CEO initially supporting this action and then having to retract and apologize. This separate event, years later, highlights the same flaw as the previous example, that of treating customers poorly and not valuing them as individuals.

United Passenger, Dr. David Dao, thrown off plane

IMPACT

Many can relate to these unfortunate incidents. Airlines in the United States have clearly been focusing on different issues than treating their customers right. In both examples, we see the delayed and flatfooted response of United. Taylor Guitars, by contrast, jumped at the opportunity to replace the guitar and become the hero and silver lining of the first incident. In the second, other airlines quickly announced changes in policy, while United was stumbling to determine an appropriate response. Eventually, it too released policy changes to avoid a repeat incident. With these two incidents, more than five years apart, it's hard to understand a brand like United failing to act in a more savvy and expedient nature.

LESSON LEARNED: PERFORMANCE FAILURES CAN BECOME INFAMOUS AND EVERLASTING.

A GIFT GONE WRONG

When Apple went too far

When the most valuable brand in the world partners with, arguably, one of the biggest rock bands in the world, what could go wrong? Following the automatic distribution of a new U2 album to every iTunes account holder in 2014, few could have predicted the resulting backlash. Fueled by Twitter and a feeling of permissions exceeded, Apple responded by publishing a message and a method that reversed the "gift" to those who wished it to be removed.

IMPACT

The same week that this blunder occurred, Apple CEO Tim Cook went out of his way to make clear Apple's position of distance with respect to storing and leveraging user information (e.g., ApplePay and Healthkit). Despite seemingly good intentions, the desire of both these brands (Apple and U2) to make history for creating the largest album release exceeded their brands' permissions. Although free, some users felt encroached upon (or violated) with material appearing on their personal devices that they neither requested nor preferred. The takeaway here is that even free gifts sent to the personal devices must be considered more carefully in the future—especially during the week when Apple unveiled its most "intimate" product: the Apple Watch.

LESSON LEARNED: DON'T ABUSE YOUR POWERS

SOCIAL PLATFORM BREAKUPS

Foursquare breakup

How do you break up with a social media platform full of friends and family, or the place with all your business connections, or the tool that collects and rewards you for your favorite hangouts and social habits? Engineered to keep you following, linking, and liking, these platforms are continually tinkering to make users' sessions sticky and commercially viable. But sometimes those tweaks, married with general user fatigue, can go terribly wrong, and the impact can create a permanent indifference among a brand's users.

One of the best articulations of indifference is evidenced in this article of a break-up letter to Foursquare. It starts with "Oh, Foursquare. We're breaking up. It's not me. It's you…" and ends with "Sincerely, A Former Lover." In between, you can see an edited emotional transcription of passionate brand intimacy moving toward complete indifference.

"Oh, Foursquare. We're breaking up. It's not me. It's you. I know this may come as something as a surprise; after all, I've known you longer than I've known my wife and been with you more places...

...But now, now you've failed at everything you were once good at. You didn't stay true to your roots. You doubted yourself in your middle age. ...After all, you're the only company I trust to out-Foursquare Foursquare, and with the whole existing rich database to draw on, it was possible you could. I reluctantly installed Swarm...

...But then Swarm sucked. It crashed. All. The. Time. On iOS. On Android. A product that willfully refused to perform its core task. A pencil unwilling to write...

Instead, you just shoved avid users into a shitty app that crashes all the time. There's only so many "Sorry, Swarm has quit" messages a guy can take. So, after 3,044 check-ins and 68 badges, your user #11471 is throwing in the towel. Goodbye.

Sincerely, A Former Lover"[122]

Another consumer in a similar state offered this gem in describing a painful Facebook breakup:

"I'm done with you, too. I hate the feeling I get when I'm comparing myself to my peers. Why is it so wrong to dislike using Facebook? Do I really have to post every thought, urge, feeling, and experience to you? Why is it necessary to share my experiences with you? I like that you help me stay connected to people, but at the same time, I feel like we (as a society) have lost the ability to appreciate good, old-fashioned face-to-face communication…"

From our online community, we found this succinct break up:

"I can't keep forgiving a brand for constant mistakes, for invading my privacy and for clearly not understanding me. Bye, bye!"

U.S. consumer

IMPACT

Owners and enablers of social communities, like those elected to run our real communities, have responsibilities and obligations to their constituents.

LESSON LEARNED: DON'T BE PERCEIVED AS AN OVERLORD; FACTOR IN STAKEHOLDERS AND ADVANCE WITH CARE AND CONSIDERATION.

3-3

BUILDING MORE INTIMATE BRANDS

R

ESSENCE   STORY   EXPERIENCE

YOUR
BRAND

YOUR
STAKEHOLDERS

The most common question we receive when we discuss brand intimacy with marketers all over the world, is, "How can I build a more intimate brand?" Executives from companies of every size see the intuitive clarity of the approach yet their needs can vary depending on their brand's evolution or state.

In some cases it is retooling an existing brand, in others it's creating something completely new. In all cases, the principles involve leveraging emotion as the core of any brand foundation.

Building a more intimate brand requires ongoing commitment and focus. To help guide the process we've developed a straightforward framework that encompasses all marketing activities. This includes strategy and communications through to design and activation, across disciplines and divisions with both internal and external partners and contributors. Think of this framework in three levels, each nested within each other in a Russian doll-like configuration. These three levels are Essence, Story, and Experience. Taken as a whole, they encompass all facets of brand building across strategic, visual, verbal, and activation-oriented activities.

Brands have used this framework to gauge their gaps and to align the investments and effort required. Each level can contain multiple activities which we will provide a summary of here.

ESSENCE

Intimate brands start with a strong foundation or core. We call this essence. Here is where the brand is constructed for greater impact by creating an ownable force of attraction and connection. This is home to research and insights, naming, brand strategy, architecture, visual identity, and design system for a brand. Utilizing established brand intimacy principles, brands are oriented toward their users, positioned to foster an emotional bond and designed to be distinctive. This aids in instinctive and fast decision making, mirroring the way people process information and strengthens a brand's ability to attract users.

When crafting a brand's positioning or promise we begin with an emotional spectrum. This is one of our primary tools to ensure we are building an emotional brand from its foundation. Brands typically tend to focus on the bottom half of the spectrum, emphasizing their rational and literal associations. This focus includes trying to highlight what they do (descriptive), what they sell (products/services), or how they do it (process).

ARCHITECT YOUR BRAND

ESSENCE

INSIGHTS

VALUE PROPOSITION

NAME / IDENTITY

BRAND ARCHITECTURE

DESIGN - LOOK & FEEL

BRAND MANAGEMENT

When positioning an intimate brand, strive to emphasize the top half of the spectrum, highlighting who the brand is (personality), the ethos the brand is trying to deliver (experience), or the ultimate reason why the brand exists/does what it does (purpose/benefit). By orienting a brand toward the top half, we can create opportunities at the strategy level for a brand to establish strong bonds and deep connections.

PROMISE/ VALUE PROPOSITION SPECTRUM

MORE EMOTION

Why you do it

What's the experience

Who you are

How you do it

What you sell

What you are

MORE RATIONAL

ESSENCE: COMMON PITFALLS

Too often, companies let their brand essence erode over time, either by ignoring it or by not acknowledging the changing business landscape and the need for revisiting their brand and gaining or maintaining consensus. Or some brands want to revise their brand strategy but choose to neglect the visual components of their brand. Both of these components are critical and should work in concert. A new positioning with an old design does not create a compelling whole.

People make decisions based on what things say and how things look. It's important these are working in concert, toward the same goal. Limitations or lack of synergy in essence set off a chain reaction of marketing deficiencies throughout all levels of an intimate brand.

STORY

The next level of building an intimate brand is called story. This level plays an increasingly important role as brands engage in more reciprocity and social marketing channels. Brand content in today's omni-channel universe demands a strong narrative that connects audiences to a brand in emotionally driven ways. Leveraging the right mix of compelling archetypes can be a key way to provide emotional direction and content orientation. Brands charged by powerful narratives will foster greater engagement and relevance. Story can encompass social media, integrated campaigns, creative content and thought leadership.

In a fluid marketplace, brands armed with a strong story level can pivot, react and stay ahead of the competition. They can also initiate programs that encourage reciprocity and make users feel involved and encouraged. This is becoming increasingly vital. While almost all brands have some version of essence, not all brands have well-developed story components. A strong narrative enables segmented communications to sharing, bonding, and fusing customers, and

SHAPING A STRONG NARRATIVE

STORY

MESSAGING

THOUGHT LEADERSHIP

CONTENT

INTEGRATED CAMPAIGNS

MEDIA

both engages and delights those connected to the brand, helping them deepen their relationships and move to the next stage of intimacy.

In the case of building the story component, look at the importance of creating powerful content and determining the optimal ways to share and distribute it to maximize its cost, effectiveness and engagement. This involves architecting the content: what to lead with, what to support, how the content gets segmented (by audience, geography, industry, etc.). Then it's important to determine taxonomy: creating a technical plan for supporting content objectives with metadata and consistent nomenclature to enhance search results and build user familiarity with the campaign or language used. Last, consider merchandising: how the content gets segmented and shared. From enticing bite-size bits of information to infographics to video and long form material, how can the merchandising potential of this material be maximized? Where can dialogue be invited? Intimacy can be an important filter, both to help you build strong content and to make content decisions in terms of prioritization.

CONTENT PREREQUISITES

HIERARCHY

TAXONOMY

MERCHANDISING

STORY: COMMON PITFALLS

A lack of story-related offerings often suggest a brand may have a limited tone, manner, and personality, basically not much distinctiveness in the market. Whether it's ideas consumers connect with or valuable information for a business audience, without story, brands will have a hard time engaging with their users and deepening reciprocal relationships.

EXPERIENCE

The final part of the framework in shaping a more intimate brand is the most expansive and encompassing; it is where the rubber meets the road between brand and its stakeholders. It is one thing to have a strong brand in theory; the experience phase is where the brand lives in practice. This includes all the physical, environmental, and digital worlds where a brand exists. The goal is orchestrating an elevated experience that centers on delivering more personalized, memorable and enhanced moments, in more places, across more devices. Whether physical or digital touchpoints, stakeholders of the brand are increasingly attuned to the consistency and overall caliber of brands. With this greater scrutiny comes less tolerance for weak retail experiences, poor customer service, or product or services failures. Further compounding the challenge, marketing channels today are becoming more fractured, and they are evolving, which forces brands to adapt and embed themselves with greater frequency and efficiency.

ORCHESTRATING ELEVATED, PERSONALIZED, MEMORABLE MOMENTS

USER EXPERIENCE

TECHNOLOGY

INTERFACE DESIGN

DIGITAL PLATFORMS   EXPERIENCE

EVENTS

ENVIRONMENTS

Look at the customer's journey across multiple touchpoints to map a carefully considered range of experiences through integrated programs and initiatives.

Here, understanding your Brand Intimacy Quotient score can be invaluable. You can see what archetypes you've been associated with, which stages you're effectively building bonds and which users (male, female, old, young, income levels) you're most successful at connecting with. From there, a more detailed journey mapping can focus on the brand's ability to engage and delight customers more effectively and align the growing and complex universe of touchpoints. From how the infrastructure can better support the desired outcomes, to the tools and processes that bring the experience to life, orchestrate synergized experiences that are designed to deepen bonds and encourage reciprocity. Here it's key to dimension and bring to life appropriate triggers like select archetypes, key messages, visual cues, design components, personalized communications, and opportunities for dialogue.

USER EXPERIENCE ORCHESTRATION

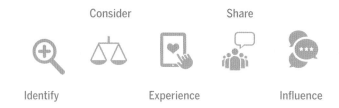

Consider   Share

Identify   Experience   Influence

EXPERIENCE: COMMON PITFALLS

It may be surprising to highlight that often well executed brand experiences are limited by antiquated infrastructure and processes. Uninspired materials distributed across channels that are not frequently updated or optimized worsen the impact. There is a lack of creativity with touchpoints that influence behavior. Often we find diminished attention to detail, or else few campaigns that attempt to engage customers in new ways. These are all missed opportunities to build dialogue and foster relationships to improve your brand intimacy performance.

3-4

THE BRAND INTIMACY PLATFORM

Marketers today are facing increasing pressures to demonstrate a return on investment and the ability to be seen within their organizations as in control of the brand. Truly intimate brands start by excelling inside of organizations first. A strong, unified culture aligned to a compelling vision and a clear articulation of the brand promise is the priority before even trying to convert prospects into customers.

In these dynamic and evolving times there is top down pressure within the leadership of companies to create tangible results in quarters versus years. Financial measures increasingly supersede more intangibles ones that are associated with maintaining strong brands like goodwill, equity or even brand value. Without a meaningful measurement for your brand like the Brand Intimacy Quotient, the actual bonds formed with customers are left to be measured in only transactional ways.

It is against this void that we built the Brand Intimacy Platform, software designed to create cohesion and power for your brand and further build bonds across your organization. The platform has evolved through an amalgamation of disparate tools used by Fortune 1,000 companies that spanned numerous industries such as finance, healthcare, automotive, real estate, technology and consumer goods. We've created a battle-ready suite of functionality that solves disparate items like digital asset management (DAM), brand management and intranet content management. Over the years, the tools have integrated into a variety of enterprise environments and have been customized for the diverse needs of brands of every scale and type. We observed that as cloud-based platforms proliferate and the landscape continues to get crowded, software that unites a marketing organization and its community of internal and external stakeholders remains limited. Armed with our new paradigm of brand intimacy, we sought to align our various distinct tools and features and unite them into a powerful platform focused on building stronger bonds for the entire marketing ecosystem of stakeholders. Implementing and using software that delivers the glue for managing and deploying brands depends on several key criteria. Next, we detail each tenet with some support examples. These are important to consider as you tackle ways to maintain, build and advance your intimate brand with a platform like the one we describe or with other solutions.

INTEGRATION

The biggest initial barrier marketers typically face is one of technical infrastructure within organizations. The degree of flexibility and openness to adding platforms within a company creates, at a minimum, tension between marketing and technology teams, and at worst, a major struggle.

BRAND INTIMACY PLATFORM

The Brand Intimacy Platform is built to integrate primarily with broad enterprise-wide systems like Oracle, SAP and Microsoft (and others) that establish the critical technical foundation for many companies. Secondarily, the platform is designed to also integrate with the myriad of other cloud solutions that may be in use in areas of the sales and marketing technology landscape including Salesforce, HubSpot or DAM systems like DropBox, Box or other web technologies like Google services and Adobe Cloud. Success for marketers today lies in the ability to build an ecosystem that is nimble and flexible with both the large technology super systems that run companies and the many niche and department-level tools that specific teams favor. As the landscape of solutions, platforms, and technologies continues to evolve and accelerate over time, the Brand Intimacy Platform remains flexible, open and adaptable.

MEASUREMENT AND INSIGHTS

While integration is key to the set-up and running of the platform, measurement and insights are the dynamic data that delivers brand performance feedback, predicative opportunities, and validation. The Brand Intimacy Platform unites a range of research and marketing data, tools and repositories. Against what can be a massive vault of material, marketers need effective sorting, filtering and search tools to find information in fast, visual and intuitive ways. An editorial layer is an option for some clients, that bring the insights more to life in a series of infographics, short blurbs, imagery and keywords.

Executives are continually searching for a sure thing—the silver bullet solution that will generate the next big increase in awareness, trial, or sales. In our practice working with Fortune 1,000 brands, and in discussions with marketers that represent the top ranking intimate brands, the conversation frequently involves understanding how they can reliably predict brand intimacy. We built a tool as part of the platform that helps predict the impact of potential marketing efforts on a brand's intimacy quotient. This predictive model, or simulator, lets marketers and researchers alter their archetype or stage ratings to see how those changes could impact their overall intimacy score. This tool gives us a model for scenario planning which is extremely valuable when trying to develop new communication platforms, discover new ways to attract customers, or determine which brand to leverage when optimizing a brand or product architecture portfolio.

The simulator uses the model as a flexible desktop tool that can render scenarios by changing a brand's archetype scores. Each increase or decrease in a particular archetype score will visualize the real-time impact on brand intimacy stages and overall quotient scores.

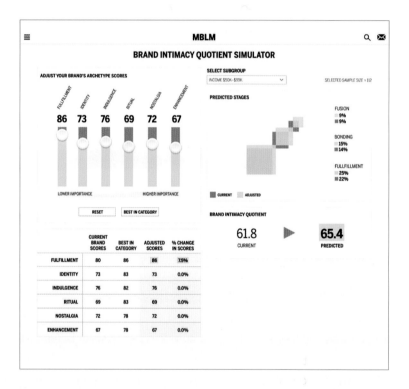

Naturally, this type of simulation is only possible with brands that have existing intimacy data or are using a proxy brand for comparative purposes. We are regularly surprised to see the impact that archetypes can have on more intimate brands. The combination of strong archetype pairs can also dramatically alter the score in surprising ways. The simulator was designed to visualize, test and explore a variety of scenarios before making marketing commitments.

Predicting brand intimacy can be as important as building a real-time tracking tool to measure it. Our clients are eager to understand and track in real-time the emotional performance of their brands. So, to complement our other research sources, we began to mine social media data to reveal additional current, candid, and comprehensive insights. According to Pew Research, more than 74 percent of all adult Internet users engage with social media, giving us a potentially deep and varied pool of data on brands and their users.[123]

Social listening and sentiment tracking tools paired with appropriate algorithms provide an effective means for marketers to survey the social web. Our aim is to provide up-to-the-minute feedback on a product, an athlete, or politician's positive, neutral, or negative sentiment, and much more, by essentially aggregating social platforms, search portals, blogs, or news sites, and factoring what people write, comment, or share about a brand. We are building on sentiment by gathering verbatim comments, shared/posted images and even emoticons, which we believe all provide important emphasis or tone to the commentary.

By leveraging the influence and scale of social media, we are now adding the real-time tracking of emotional currency for a brand as a way to gauge market reactions and/or predict future performance.

COMMUNITY

A company's internal culture plays a pivotal role in the success of any brand. The stronger the brand intimacy a brand builds with its customers, you can expect to see a cohesive team working within the organization delivering on their brand promise, meaning marketing community features are at the heart of the Brand Intimacy Platform. First and most importantly, access is provided to audiences within and outside the company that are all working with or on marketing and communication efforts. Agencies, consultants, production vendors and partners are some of the typically invited stakeholders and the platform is the central destination for all those involved in building the brand.

A timeline driven 'wall' is the home screen experience to the platform which promotes the news and daily information flow related to the company. As it evolves in small and big ways the "pulse" home screen creates a manifestation of the people, events and achievements of the brand over time and a more engaging intranet feature.

Beyond the screen showcasing the living and breathing brand in action, the content of the platform forms the connective tissue for the community. This encompasses everything from essential guidance and key assets, to detailed explanations and rationale behind the strategies, design and activations that form the brand management core of the brand. It is relevant for everyone from the casual visitor looking for a simple asset or template, to the power user who needs to be fully conversant in the essence of the brand. The platform is designed to be visually beautiful, customized for the brand in all of the interface elements, and easy to navigate.

BEHAVIOR

Whether creating a new brand or transforming an existing one, building more intimate bonds with your customers requires some degree of transformation in the methods and priorities that drove your previous marketing efforts. This transformation demands new or augmented goals and motivations, and ultimately new outcomes from your marketing and communication teams, agencies, partners and vendors. That's why the Brand Intimacy Platform is engineered to encourage on-brand behavior and strong bonds internally. From the pulse home screen that first greets users, the goal is to promote commenting and sharing. Social collaboration is central to the user experience. Some clients choose to go further having an internal awards section that allows member participation through voting and recognition of awards for excellence and best practices.

On a more pragmatic level, a robust help desk feature creates a valuable way to govern brand requirements. This part of the platform creates a streamlined workflow that allows different departments like marketing, sales and legal to review and comment on materials prior to release. Our clients have saved millions of dollars on this functionality alone, gaining stronger compliance and controls while identifying weak areas to the brand or the marketing organization they need to address. Once the Brand Intimacy Platform becomes established and engrained within a company, we see a greatly elevated attitude and performance around the brand. The platform resolves and clarifies ambiguities and unknowns related to the brand, thus the time saved by no longer educating or policing can be used toward solving more creative marketing and strategic issues.

As the brand projects outward or gets activated on screens and environments, the Brand Intimacy Platform performs a critical function in improving and transforming the way the brands sells itself. The platform is designed to empower sales and communication teams to effectively engage with their audiences using the latest content that is easily updated and centrally managed. Whether in intimate iPad demonstrations, on touch screen kiosks, or across massive video walls in sales/retail environments, the platform delivers a compelling selling experience of the brand's products and services to customers of all kinds. One of the most powerful aspects of the platform is that every action or follow-up is measured, tracked and can be integrated with sales or CRM tools. A dashboard of internal user activities as well as the status of kiosks or screens in use is summarized in a detailed dashboard, enabling a clear perspective on who's utilizing tools, what's connecting with customers and what can be further optimized.

IMPACT

The relationships or bonds your brand forms are dynamic and ever-evolving. As we have been detailing, to thrive in marketing today, you need a software marketing platform that effectively manages, connects and enables your intimate brand.

For IT groups that are responsible for technology infrastructure, brand platforms have to deliver low overhead, ease of deployment and a modular suite of functionality that can be scaled up or down. In companies large or small, platforms for marketing are typically on the lower end of priorities. Therefore, how easily or effectively marketing tools can be integrated plays a critical factor in their success.

Most importantly, software for creating brand intimacy is only as effective as the human processes and outcomes they enhance or improve. Every second of every day, a brand is either building or diluting its intimacy with stakeholders.

The goal of our marketing platform is to help teams interpret and guide the nuances and evolution of the brand over time. A software platform is an essential tool when trying to advance an intimate brand, particularly across geographies and divisions.

LOOKING AHEAD

In Chapter 1.5, Discovery, one of the key findings is that technology can either enable or diminish brand intimacy. As technology continues to advance, the impact on how brands are built, managed and ultimately experienced requires that we ensure technology is working effectively to build stronger bonds and relationships.

This is both an exciting and daunting possibility. We are living in a time of profound innovation of artificial intelligence and automation. Connected appliances bring virtual assistants into our homes while in business some of the biggest challenges we face regarding healthcare or finance are now the responsibility of computers to solve. For us in marketing, we seek automation techniques that scan and react to our online behavior. Media has become programmatic and at the time of this writing, Adobe just announced an experimental program called Sensei that uses machine learning to create graphics and web layouts. There are already online tools that create unique names from word parts, apps that generate logos from sketches and programs that can write long form copy that is indistinguishable from human authors. We can anticipate that every aspect of the brand creation and marketing process will soon evolve from being aided by computers to being mainly created and managed by them.

What will remain constant, irrespective of the role or impact that technology will play, is our indelible need to connect and bond with people, products and places. We will be forever drawn to the products and services that we identify with or that enhance, fulfill or indulge us. We will be won over by nostalgia and form strong habits through ritual. Like we do with the people in our lives that we bond with, we'll evolve our relationships with brands from sharing to bonding and in select cases, fusing, where we'll be inexorably linked and fully co-identified. The Brand Intimacy Platform is the technology solution for the new paradigm. It can be a compass for how marketers today and in the future will evolve the brands we make, use, buy and treasure.

The Brand Intimacy Platform is the technology solution for today's new paradigm in marketing. The platform helps marketers harness their entire stakeholder ecosystem to evolve their brand to create stronger bonds. Companies that have leveraged the platform have changed how their customers feel, buy and ultimately treasure the brand.

IMPLICATIONS

Top intimate brands outperform the S&P and Fortune 500 for revenue, profit and longevity.

Intimate brands command greater price premiums.

Common pitfalls for brands today most often relate to not being agile, not having a customer-centric perspective, overstepping and overreach.

Building stronger and more intimate brands happens through powerful essence, story and experience.

Software will play an increasingly vital role in fueling intimate brands. Our Brand Intimacy Platform enables and optimizes the entire marketing ecosystem.

CONCLUSION

THE POWER OF INTIMATE BRANDS

The marketplace is constantly evolving, and as new technologies and a dynamic consumer base continue to change how brands are designed and perceived, we knew that a revision of marketing's fundamental principles was long overdue. Rational-based strategies; artificial testing approaches based on behavioral hierarchies that don't reflect the real buying process; the assumption that awareness and consideration lead to purchases—these concepts, while not necessarily obsolete, are almost certainly outdated with how consumers interact with, buy and use brands.

We now understand that the biggest indicator of purchase is how we *feel* about a brand. Feelings in general are a tremendous area of opportunity, and by creating brands that people connect and relate to—brands that tell a compelling story in a simple straightforward way—marketers can both take advantage of and create new opportunities. Decision making is instinctive and emotional. The question is, how can marketers leverage these new insights to their advantage? It will clearly require keeping things short, sweet, and impactful.

Is brand intimacy easy? No. Does it necessitate changing a lot of conventional approaches? Probably. Does it make sense? Clearly. Does it make *business* sense? **Definitely.**

It is our hope that this book gets people thinking about the actual relationships people have with brands…and, in being a relationship, how it can be reciprocal and engaging. What must brands do to deepen bonds with consumers? How can they invite dialogue and engagement? Most people think only of how brands can attract and sell, not how they can participate in a relationship and deepen bonds with people.

Our biggest thrill is helping companies better understand and realize their intimate brand potential. From assessing opportunities and developing corresponding marketing strategies through to design and execution, there are literally hundreds of ways, both big and small, that companies can improve their effectiveness in creating brand intimacy.

Ultimately, companies need their brands to drive tangible results. Therefore, it makes the best sense to concentrate efforts on those areas that have proven to show results. When we see new partners and customers being drawn to a brand as it lays claim to new emotional territory, we know that what we're doing *works*.

Whether a company is a small start-up or a massive multi-billion-dollar global conglomerate, brand intimacy can create incremental or transformational improvements in your marketing efforts. We encourage all brands to build bonds, link to emotions, and amplify their relevance through increased intimacy.

Just as with any relationship, the more you put in, the more you get out.

BRAND INTIMACY

2010

2011

2012

2013

2014   2015   2016   2017

Appendix

**EXPLORE THE BRAND INTIMACY STUDY FOR
DEEPER INSIGHTS AND FINDINGS.**

VISIT: mblm.com/brandintimacy

COMPREHENSIVE COUNTRY REPORTS FOR THE U.S., MEXICO AND THE UAE

**INTERACTIVE RANKING TOOL WITH DETAILED BRAND
PROFILES DASHBOARD FEATURING:**

**BRAND INTIMACY QUOTIENT SCORES
INDUSTRY RANKINGS AND COMPARISONS
DEMOGRAPHIC CUTS BY AGE, INCOME AND GENDER
NET PROMOTER SCORE
FREQUENCY OF USE
CAN'T LIVE WITHOUT PERCENTAGES**

10 WAYS TO ASSESS THE INTIMACY OF YOUR BRAND

The purpose of these 10 considerations is to provide marketers with a clearer set of questions to narrow down and diagnose clear gaps in their brand performance. These questions, in whole or in part, can play a pivotal role in enhancing your brand and moving you toward creating more emotionally charged, emotive bonds.

Brands are ever-evolving and culturally driven. When done right, they can predict and lead the business. Yet too often, brands are seen as expenses to the business instead of the glue between the company and its stakeholders. Like any relationship you want to foster or improve, underinvesting in these bonds creates a greater drag on the business and stunts the growth of bonds that could otherwise propel the business forward.

1

EXAMINE THE BONDS YOUR BRAND BUILDS

- Are you using yesterday's strategies to solve tomorrow's marketing problems? Or are you relying on traditional (and likely dated) methods of brand building to try and remain compelling and relevant today?

- Do you know what influences the bonds people have with your brand?

- Do you have the methods and tools to determine this bond?

We start with bonds, the foundation of intimate relationships. What this group of questions is asking is, why do people connect with your brand? What drives your brand relationships? Do you know how to measure those relationships?

2

ARTICULATE AND MOTIVATE THROUGH YOUR BRAND

- Does the essence of your brand promote or inspire intimacy with your stakeholders?

- Is your brand's essence rooted in factors that enable it to forge powerful emotional connections that drive decision making?

- Does your brand align with enduring human fundamentals best used to create connection?

- Can your brand be more relevant to audiences that matter most?

Here, we're trying to determine if your brand is based on emotion and fosters quick decision making. If your brand is not based on emotion, it is important to start here. A rational hook might have been good enough until now, but it won't optimize the brand's potential. Are you leveraging the archetypes? Which ones? How?

3

ALIGN YOUR BRAND AND YOUR CULTURAL VALUES

- Since your brand has to first establish bonds with internal stakeholders and partners, are they aligned, inspired, and ready to deliver compelling on-brand experiences?

- Do employees understand their role in building the brand?

- Do they realize they have an opportunity to evangelize through each customer interaction?

Have you created a living, breathing brand that employees can be proud of and a part of? Does your brand reflect your employees? Do they understand their role as ambassadors? Before focusing on customers, focus first on the people who influence customers. They are your defense, your offense and a clear way to give the brand a human dimension.

4

DESIGN AND COMMUNICATE FOR TODAY'S AESTHETIC SENSIBILITIES

- Does your brand's identity, messaging, and content resonate?

- Are you attracting the right audiences?

- Does your brand promote sharing, bonding, or fusing behavior to help build ultimate relationships?

- Do your materials create distinction compared with your competitors, and are they optimized for today's digital landscape?

Is your brand effectively communicating in ways that matter? Does it have a distinctive, easy-to-identify look that stands out from competitors? Is it inviting, engaging and intriguing? Is it talking to consumers in a way that suggests dialogue and relationship, or is it one-way and top down? Do you make it easy to get involved and start a relationship with your brand?

5

MANAGE YOUR BRAND AND FOSTER YOUR MARKETING COMMUNITY LIKE AN OPERATING SYSTEM

- Is your brand managed in a disciplined way, yet adaptable to changing needs or conditions?

- Are you supporting your marketing and communications community effectively?

- Are you striking the right balance between engaging your marketing community and mandating to them?

- Can you identify where, when, and why your brand succeeds or fails to meet expectations?

An intimate brand needs the right tools in place to act quickly, speak compellingly, and create crafted moments. Are you using state of the art tools so that your marketing team can deliver what is required on time and on budget? Are you sharing best practices and innovations? Have you assessed what platforms are most successful and why?

6

DRIVE YOUR BRAND TO INFORM AND PLEASE CUSTOMERS IN EVERY INTERACTION

- Are you demonstrating your brand's value or offer through effective content and truly integrated campaigns?

- Do you have an optimized media mix?

- Are your methods delivering consistent experiences that resonate?

- Can you identify the areas of weakness in your activation?

Are you aligned to where your customers go? Do you promote your brand in the right channels with the right content to maximize their interest and engagement? Are you investing in content that adds value or are you relying on customers to create content? Are you communicating with customers frequently enough (or too frequently)?

7

USE THE PROLIFERATION OF DEVICES AND PLATFORMS AS AN ALLY

- Is your brand in enough channels or in the right ones?

- Have you developed ways to leverage the ubiquity of device usage to become a more valuable part of customers' personal and work lives?

- Are you balancing traditional and emerging platforms to broaden your audiences?

Are you experimenting across channels? Do you have multiple trials and campaigns going on at the same time to test new ideas to build stronger bonds? Have you optimized across devices to make it easier for your customer to be delighted to be interacting with you?

8

SEE YOUR BRAND AS A COMMUNITY AND YOURSELF AS THE ACTIVITIES COORDINATOR

- Are you discovering and embracing the communities that your customers frequent?

- Can you create compelling content for these communities?

- Are you finding ways to engage, dialogue with, and influence consumers, in addition to selling?

- Is your customer engagement elusive?

What value are you creating for customers? People are busy. Good content gets noticed. Promotions, coupons, and giveaways are table stakes. Are you identifying important new ways to create compelling material? How are you building communities? Do you follow your own brand? Do your employees? What kind of meaningful dialogues are you fostering?

9

DON'T LET THE DELUGE OF DATA DROWN OUT THE SIGNAL FROM THE NOISE

- Have your analytics been aligned with the right marketing goals?

- Are you measuring traditional and emerging aspects of brand performance?

- Are you measuring and benchmarking the depth and intensity of your customer relationships?

- Does your brand performance measure up?

With the proliferation of data, what are you measuring and how often? Are you pleased with your performance? Are you testing or benchmarking increased emotional connection with customers? Do you measure traditional and emerging channels differently? What are your objectives? Are they short-term gains or long-term wins? Would you be more successful moving customers from sharing to bonding or trying to build more fused relationships?

10

CREATE AND SUSTAIN ULTIMATE BRAND RELATIONSHIPS

- Are your stakeholders and your brand co-identified?

- Is there positive emotion behind customer behavior toward your brand?

- Are you fulfilling the expectations of all your audiences?

- Do your efforts correlate to real business performance?

Are you building an intimate brand? Are you measuring bonds? How can you create relationships, not transactions? Are you pleased with your performance? How are you continuing to deepen customer bonds? Are these efforts improving your bottom line?

REFERENCES

Endnotes

1   Story, L. (January 2007). "Anywhere the Eye Can See, It's Likely to See an Ad," http://www.nytimes.com/2007/01/15/business/media/15everywhere.html?.

2   Bolman, Chris. "How to Win Anyone's Attention." Percolate, Sept 25, 2014. https://blog.percolate.com/2014/09/how-to-win-anyones-attention/.

3   Chen, Y. (March 2015). "84 Percent of Millennials Don't Trust Traditional Advertising," http://www.clickz.com/clickz/news/.

4   Egan, John, "18 statistics that marketers need to know about millennials," LeadsCon, Jan 22, 2015. http://www.leadscon.

5   Asknert, S. (April 2015). "Nielsen study - Global Trust in Advertising 2015," https://company.trnd.com/en/blog/nielsen-study-global-trust-in-advertising-2015.

6   "State of the American Consumer: Insights for Business Leaders," Gallup 2014.

7   Zorfas, Alan and Leemon, Don. "An Emotional Connection Matters More than Customer Satisfaction," Harvard Business Review, Aug 29, 2016.

8   Ibid.

9   Murray, Peter N. Ph.D., "How Emotions Influence What We Buy," Psychology Today. https://www.psychologytoday.com/blog/inside-the-consumer-mind/201302/how-emotions-influence-what-we-buy.

10   "Cisco Visual Networking Index: Global Mobile Data Traffic Forecast Update," 2002–2017, February 6, 2013, http://cisco.com/en/US/solutions/collateral/ns341/ns525/ns537/ns705/ns827/white_paper_c11-520862.html.

11   IBM Institute for Business Value, "CMOs and CIOs," 2011, http://public.dhe.ibm.com/common/ssi/ecm/en/gbe03513usen/GBE03513USEN.PDF.

12   "What Is 'Haptic Feedback'?," MobileBurn, 2013. http://www.mobileburn.com/definition.jsp?term=haptic+feedback.

13   Dublon, G. and Paradiso, J. A., "Extra Sensory Perception," Scientific American, July 2014. Web: Aug. 1, 2014. http://www.scientificamerican.com/article/how-a-sensor-filled-world-will-change-human-consciousness/.

14   Ibid.

15   Ibid.

16   Ibid.

17   Geirland, J., "Go With the Flow," Wired, Issue 4.09, Sept. 1996. Web: http://archive.wired.com/wired/archive/4.09/czik.html.

18   "Introduction to Google Glass," The Guardian, June 2, 2014. https://www.theguardian.com/guardian-masterclasses/introduction-to-google-glass-michael-rosenblum-digital-course.

19   "Watch," Apple, 2014. https://www.apple.com/watch/overview/.

20   Zuckerberg, M., Posts, Facebook, March 25, 2014.
Web: https://www.facebook.com/zuck/posts/10101319050523971.

21   Carnegie, D., "The Rule of Balance—Logical Mind vs. Emotional Heart,"
Westside Toastmasters, http://westsidetoastmasters.com/resources/laws_
persuasion/chap14.html.

22   The Behavioral Economics Guide 2014, edited by Alain Samson. http://www.
behavioraleconomics.com/BEGuide2014.pdf.

23   Damasio, Antonio, The Feeling of What Happens, Houghton Mifflin Harcourt
Publishing Company, 1999.

24   Kahneman, Daniel, "Thinking Fast and Slow," Farrar, Straus and Giroux, 2011.

25   Ibid.

26   Haidt, Jonathan, The Righteous Mind: Why Good People are Divided by Religion
and Politics. Penguin Random House 2012.

27   Ibid.

28   The Behavioral Economics Guide 2014, edited by Alain Samson.
http://www.behavioraleconomics.com/BEGuide2014.pdf.

29   *Ibid.*

30   "Net Promoter." Wikipedia. March 16, 2017. https://en.wikipedia.org/wiki/Net_
Promoter.

31   Reichheld, F. (December 2003). "One Number You Need to Grow".
Harvard Business Review. https://en.wikipedia.org/wiki/Net_Promoter
- cite_note-OneNumber-3.

32   "What is Net Promoter," https://www.netpromoter.com, 2017.

33   "Walker Loyalty Matrix," Walker, 2013, http://www.walkerinfo.com/docs/WP-The-
Walker-Loyalty-Matrix.pdf.

34   Giddens, Nancy, "Brand Loyalty," Iowa State University extension and Outreach,
Aug 2010. http://www.extension.iastate.edu/agdm/wholefarm/html/c5-54.html.

35   *M. Uncles, A.S.C. Ehrenberg, and K. Hammond, "Patterns of Buyer Behavior:
Regularities, Models, and Extensions," Marketing Science, volume 14, number 3,
1995, pp. G71–G78.*

36   Ibid.

37   Sharp, Byron, How Brands Grow. Oxford University Press, March, 2010, p. x1.

38   Marsden, Paul, "How Brands Grow [Speed Summary] Brand Genetics, Nov, 2012
http://brandgenetics.com/how-brands-grow-speed-summary/.

39   "BrandAsset Valuator" Young & Rubicam Group, 2003, http://www.yrbav.com/
about_bav/bav%20blue%20book.pdf.

40   Interbrand, "Methodology," http://interbrand.com/best-brands/best-global-
brands/methodology/.

41   Treacy, Michael and Wiersema, Fred., "Customer Intimacy and Other Value
Disciplines," Harvard Business Review, January-February 1993, www.a3o.be/
materialen-en-links/images/.../treacywiersema.pdf.

42   Ibid.

43   Ibid.

44   Treacy, Michael and Wiersema, Fred, The Discipline of Market Leaders, Addison-Wesley, 1995.

45   Ibid.

46   Abramovich, Giselle, "How Brands De ne Engagement," Digiday, August 29, 2012, http://www.digiday.com/brands/how-brands- define-engagement/.

47   Gensler, "2013 Brand Engagement Survey: The Emotional Power of Brands," 2013. http://www.gensler.com/uploads/document/354/ le/2013_Brand_Engagement_Survey_10_21_2013.pdf.

48   "How Do I Know a Lovemark?," Saatchi & Saatchi, 2013, http://www.lovemarks.com/index.php?pageID=20020.

49   "The Lovemark Pro ler," Saatchi & Saatchi, 2013, http://www.lovemarks.com/index.php?pageID=20031.

50   Ibid.

51   "Apple," Saatchi & Saatchi, 2013, http://www.lovemarks.com/index.php?pageID= 20015&lovemarkid=135.

52   Gobé, M. Emotional branding: The new paradigm for connecting brands to people. New York: Allworth Press, 2009.

53   Scott, Andrea Diahann Gay, Relationship advertising: Investigating the strategic appeal of intimacy (disclosure) in services marketing. University of South Florida, 2004.

54   Ibid.

55   Ibid.

56   Miller, Rowland & Perlman, Daniel, Intimate Relationships (5th ed.). McGraw-Hill, 2008.

57   Ibid.

58   James, W. (1890). "The Principles of Psychology". http://psychclassics.yorku.ca/James/Principles/prin10.htm.

59   Cardillo, M. (August 1998). "Intimate Relationships: Personality Development Through Interaction During Early Life". http://www.personalityresearch.org/papers/cardillo.html.

60   Ibid.

61   Ibid.

62   Cardillo, M. (1998). Intimate relationships: personality development through interaction during early life. Retrieved: http://www.personalityresearch.org/papers/cardillo.html.

63   Sternberg, R. J. (1986) A triangular theory of love. Psychological Review, 93. https://en.wikipedia.org/wiki/Triangular_theory_of_love.

64   Ibid.

65   65 McLeod, S. A., "Erik Erikson—Psychosocial Stages," Simply Psychology, 2008, http://www.simplypsychology.org/Erik-Erikson.html.

66   Ibid.

67   Evans, Richard I., Dialogue with Erik Erikson, Harper & Row, New York, 1967, p.48.

68   Maintenance of Relationships, 5-Stage George Levinger model, 1980, Integrated SocioPsychology, http://www.integratedsocio psychology.net/Relationship_ Maintenance/5-stagemodel-George Levinger1980.html.

69   Levinger, G. (1976), A Social Psychological Perspective on Marital Dissolution. Journal of Social Issues, 32: 21–47. doi:10.1111/j.1540-4560.1976. tb02478.x

70   Scott, A. "Relationship advertising: Investigating the strategic appeal of intimacy (disclosure) in services marketing" (2004). Graduate Theses and Dissertations. scholarcommons.usf.edu/etd/124

71   Ibid.

72   Laurenceau, J. P., "Intimacy as Interpersonal Process: the Importance of Self-Disclosure, Partner Disclosure, and Perceived Partner Responsive in Interpersonal Exchanges," Researchgate.net https://www.researchgate.net/publication/ 13685624_Intimacy_as_an_Interpersonal_Process_the_Importance_of_ Self-Disclosure_Partner_Disclosure_and_Perceived_Partner_Responsiveness_in_ Interpersonal_Exchanges.

73   Ibid.

74   Scott, A. "Relationship advertising: Investigating the strategic appeal of intimacy (disclosure) in services marketing" (2004). http://scholarcommons.usf.edu/cgi/ viewcontent.cgi?article= 2240&context=etd.

75   Ibid.

76   Scott, Andrea Diahann Gay, Relationship advertising: Investigating the strategic appeal of intimacy (disclosure) in services marketing. University of South Florida, 2004.

77   Golden, Beverly, "The Four Faces of Intimacy," Healthy Living, Relationships, February 8, 2012, http://intentblog.com/the-four-faces-of-intimacy/.

78   Evans, Richard I., Dialogue with Erik Erikson, New York: Harper & Row, 1967, p. 48.

79   Ibid.

80   Booker, Christopher. The Seven Basic Plots: Why We Tell Stories. London: Bloomsbury, 2006.

81   "Brand Finance Global 500 2016." Brand Finance. Feb. 2015. Web. Dec. 5, 2016. http://brandfinance.com/images/upload/global_500_2016_for_print.pdf

82   Smith, Craig. "Amazing Amazon Facts and Statistics," DMR Stats/Gadgets, Aug 30, 2016.

83   *Reinventing Retail: What Businesses Need to Know for 2015." Walker Sands Communications. Web. Nov. 18, 2015* http://www.walkersands.com/pdf/2015-future-of-retail.pdf.

84   "Financial Statements for Amazon.com, Inc." Bloomberg Business. Web. Sept. 18, 2015. http://www.bloomberg.com/research/stocks/financials/financials. asp?ticker=AMZN.

85　Kelleher, Kevin. "Amazon's Secret Weapon is Making Money Like Crazy." Time. Oct. 23, 2015. http://time.com/4084897/amazon-amzn-aws/.

86　"Newsroom: Fast Facts." WholeFoodsMarket.com. Web. Sept. 18, 2015. http://media.wholefoodsmarket.com/fast-facts/.

87　Ibid.

88　Jim Stengel, Grow: How Ideals Power Growth and Profit at the World's Greatest Companies, New York: Crown Publishing, Dec, 2011.

89　Gaille, Brandon, 20 Incredible Starbucks Statistics, Brandon Gaille.com, Nov 15, 2013.

90　Huang, Xun (Irene) and Huang, Zhongqiang (Tak), Wyer, Robert S. "Slowing, Down in the Good Old Days: The Eects of Nostalgia on Consumer Patience," Journal of Consumer Research, Vol. 43, Issue 3, October 1, 2016.

91　"LEGO Consumer Insights," InfoScout.

92　"The Brick: Annual Magazine 2010," LEGO, 2010.

93　"Picking Up the Pieces," The Economist, October 26, 2006.

94　Ibid.

95　Lindstrom, Martin. "LEGO engineered a remarkable turnaround of its business. How'd that happen?" LinkedIn, March 5, 2016.

96　Ibid.

97　Lutz, Ashley, "LEGO made 3 changes to become the world's most powerful toy company," Business Insider, May 12, 2015.

98　Brand Finance, "LEGO overtakes Ferrari as World's Most Valuable Brand," 2015.

99　About Us, Sephora.com.

100　The Pink Report 2015: The Sephora Shopper Beauty Packaging, June 2015.

101　Herich. Denis, "What is the Sephora Shopping Seeking?" Global Cosmetic Industry, September 20, 2015.

102　Laurenjohnson. "Netflix's Gilmore Girls Pop-up Coffee Shops Were a Massive Hit on Snapchat." – Adweek. Adweek, 25 Oct. 2016. Web. 09 July 2017. http://www.adweek.com/digital/netflixs-gilmore-girls-pop-coffee-shops-were-massive-hit-snapchat-174248/

103　Ibid.

104　Gaskin, Caoimhe. "5 Creative Snapchat Campaigns to Learn From." Digital Marketing Institute. Digital Marketing Institute, 05 July 2017. Web. 09 July 2017. https://digitalmarketinginstitute.com/blog/2017-5-23-5-snapchat-marketing-campaigns-to-learn-from

105　Aguis, Aaron. "The 10 Best Social Media Campaigns of 2016 So Far," Social Media Today, July 28, 2016.

106　"BMW ULTIMATE BENEFITS™." BMW Ultimate Benefits. N.p., n.d. Web. 09 July 2017. https://www.bmwusa.com/ultimate-benefits.html

107　Exclusive Benefits For 2016 BMW 7 Series Owners - BMW North America. N.p., 10 May 2016. Web. 09 July 2017. http://www.bmwusa.com/Standard/Content/Owner/7Series_UltimateBenefits.aspx

108   Tent Partners, Top 100 Most Powerful Brands of 2016.
       https://tenetpartners.com/top100/most-powerful-brands-list.html.

109   "Welcome to the Mercedes-Benz Club of America." MBCA. N.p., 12 Feb. 2016.
       Web. 09 July 2017. https://www.mbca.org/about-us

110   Ibid.

111   Schultz, Jonathan. "Carmakers form partnerships with niche brands to stand out."
       New York Times, March 11, 2016, p. 84.

112   Michelle Drew, Steve Schmith, Candan Erenguc, Bharath Gangula, "2014 Global
       Automotive Consumer Study," Auto News, https://www.autonews.com/assets/
       PDF/CA92618116.PDF.

113   Rifkin, Glenn, "How Harley Davidson Revs Its Brand," Strategy + Business, Oct 1,
       1997, http://www.strategy-business.com/article/12878?gko= aa3

114   Nudd, Tim. "Diet Coke Is Retweeting Its Biggest Fans in Suddenly Extravagant
       Ways" Adweek, September 2, 2015. http://www.adweek.com/adfreak/
       diet-coke-retweeting-its-biggest-fans-suddenly-extravagant-ways-166687

115   Sarah Coppens, Coca-Cola, Share a Coke, The Art of Good Advertising,
       October 20, 2015 https://theartofgoodadvertising.wordpress.com/2015/10/20/
       coca-cola-share-a-coke/.

116   Barrett, Rick. "Harley-Davidson cracks the millennials' code with bikes, events"
       http://www.southbendtribune.com/news/business/harley-davidson-cracks-the-
       millennials-code-with-bikes-events/article_c9ab3abf-aa9a-58c2-9443-
       8ced6f39cd21.html.

117   Hagerty, James. "Harley-Davidson's Hurdle: Attracting
       Young Motorcycle Riders" http://www.wsj.com/articles/
       can-harley-davidson-spark-a-motorcycle-counterculture-1434706201

118   "Top 10 Trusted Brands: What Brands to Male and Female Consumers Trust the
       Most?" Nielsen, Aug. 31, 2015.

119   "Decoding the Female Consumer & Brand Loyalty," Harbinger Communications,
       October 9, 2014.

120   Apple Inc. (2017). Q4 FY16 Consolidated Financial Statements. Retrieved from
       http://images.apple.com/newsroom/pdfs/Q4FY16ConsolidatedFinancial
       Statements.pdf

121   Reisinger, D. (2017, March 06). "Here's How Many iPhones Are Currently Being
       Used Worldwide." Forbes. Retrieved from http://fortune.com/2017/03/06/apple-
       iphone-use-worldwide/

122   Weekly, David E., Be Yourself https://byrslf.co/dear-foursquare-c7c441fdf25e#.
       5a7uejrcx.

123   Social Networking Fact Sheet, Pew Research Center, Dec 27, 2013, http://www.
       pewinternet.org/fact-sheets/social-networking-fact-sheet/

REFERENCES

Image Sources

1 page 5 (top): UPS logo by Paul Rand

2 page 5 (top): UPS logo by FutureBrand

3 page 5 (bottom): Various UPS rebranded touchpoints

4 page 7 (left): Intel's corporate brand and ingredient brand

5 page 7 (right): Intel's new corporate identity

6 page 9: Various rebranding American Airlines touchpoints

7 page 11: Marketing materials, The Palm

8 page 34: NPS Fred Reichheld, Bain & Company, and Satmetrix Systems

9 page 37: Walker's Loyalty Matrix, Walkerinfo.com

10 page 39: Interbrand's Brand Valuation Model, Interbrand.com

11 page 50: Maintenance of Relationships, 5 Stage George Levinger model, 1980

12 page 53: Scott, Andrea Diahann Gay, Relationship advertising: Investigating the strategic appeal of intimacy (disclosure) in services marketing. University of South Florida, 2004

13 page 55: Golden, Beverly, The Four Faces of Intimacy, BeverlyGolden.com

14 page 137: Adweek, 2016

15 page 139: Make A Wish

16 page 146: KBS Advertising, Anna Yeager, Art Director, Behance.com

17 page 147: MBCAEF.org

18 page 153 (top): MororcycleUSA.com

19 page 153 (bottom): Adweek, 2015

20 page 185: Ryan Block, Comcastic service disconnection, soundcloud.com/ryan-block-10

21 page 186: DaveCarrolMusic.com

22 page 187: The Daily Banter, 2017

23 page 188: iTunes op out, Apple.com

24 page 189: David E. Weekly, byrslf.co

25 page 243: Mike Sheehan Photography

ACKNOWLEDGEMENTS

We have had the pleasure of working on some of the most significant, interesting and unusual brands in the world. Besides providing exceptional experiences and fulfillment, this also provided us with the opportunity to advance our passion, brand intimacy.

Brand intimacy at its core is about building stronger bonds between your brand's stakeholders. We often like to say you can't start to even consider brand intimacy unless you have built these bonds with your employees first —this sounds like maybe the focus of our next book. Until then, our profound thanks to the talented team in MBLM and those we've worked with through the decades.

Our partners at MBLM who have built the global business of Brand Intimacy and without whom this book wouldn't be possible.

John Diefenbach
Claude Salzberger
William Shintani
Jae-yong Hwang
Eduardo Calderon
Amy Weick
Sidney Blank
Maria Gabriela Pulido
Kristiane Blomqvist

For his tireless design leadership, inspiration and production on the Annual Brand Intimacy Study and also the cover art of this book, layout design, direction and artwork of its contents.

Hui Min Lee

Our thanks to this brain trust that have invested their time, energy and passion to shepherd and advance the Brand Intimacy paradigm with us at different stages along our journey from inception to maturity.

Claude Salzberger
William Shintani
Jae-yong Hwang
Eduardo Calderon
Sidney Blank
Demetri Mihalakakos

Lyutha Al-Habsy
David Clover
Ziwar Majeed
Diego Kolsky
Steve Santangelo
Carrie Ruby

Thanks to our research partners Praxis Research led by Marcelo Nacht, Jay Allen and Adam Tomanelli. Sincere thanks as well to John Kearon and the team at Brain Juicer (System 1) for their efforts on the early qualitative findings.

To our colleagues that span over 15 plus years with MBLM and FutureBrand

Tess Abraham, Melisa Agúndez, Frank Alcock, Lyutha Al-Habsy, Juan Carlos Arias, Antonio Baglione, Elena Benítez, William Biondi, Kirt Blackwood, Roberto Bolaños, Renan Caguioa, Eduardo Calderón, Rena Capri, Stephanie Carroll, Rafael Carvalho, Allison Cavagnaro, Raymond Chan, Tini Chen, Joshua Choi, David Clover, Chris Connor, Kate Conrad, Emily Cottone, Michael A DaSilva, Anthony DeCosta, Oliver De La Rama, Rodrigo Díez, Larry Drury, Jean Louis Dumeu, Karim Abou El Fetouh, Jennifer Elliott, Thais Fonseca, Keith Foster, Martín García, Jeff Goldenberg, Youcef Haouatis, Kate Harvie, Anthony Herenda, Cheryl Hills, Deyan Iolov, Vera Kasper, Daniel Irizarry, Carol Jensen, Ramel Kabbani, Justin Kaczmar, Christina Kaufman, Mike Kennedy, Henry Kim, Stephanie Kim, Nadia Klein, Greg Kletsel, Ned Klezmer, Olaf Kreitz, Ashwin Kulothungun, Lynne LaCascia, John Lake, Cassandra Lane, Simon Lau, Tom Li, Regina Lomelí, Harka Lopchan, Ángel Lorenzo, Ziwar Majeed, Laverne Mars, Jillian Mascarenhas, Ryan McDonald, Scott McLean, Uzair Mohammad, Nermin Moufti, Johnny Okura, Brendan O'Neill, Tamara Petrovic, Heitor Piffer, Jason Pineres, Mallika Punwani, Frances Quirsfeld, Marco Raab, Marc Rabinowitz, Philip G Rojas, Carrie Ruby, Brendan Ryan, Prasanna Sagayaraj, Samar Samuel, Steve Santangelo, Michael Sheehan, Brian Shu, Elizabeth Sigal, Joshua Slaby, Aquiles Soledad, Juan Soto, Marc Stevenson, Saneesh Sukesan, Melisa Sumalabe, Joshua Swamy, Luke Swamy, Dimitri Theodoropoulos, Jinu Thomas, Mark Thwaites, Avrom Tobias, Andrea Vallarta, Thomas Weick, Jerome Whelan, Michael J Williams, Carol Wolf, Jeremy Yan, Carlson Yu, Joshua Yuzhe Zhao, Rony Zibara.

With profound thanks to our families and friends

Rina: To my biggest inspiration Larry Plapler, the best brander and adman in the business, Hadasa Plapler, Amelia Plapler, Dina Plapler, Earl McMahon, David McMahon, Steven McMahon, Benjamin Katz, Jackson Katz, Fran Gormley, Nigel Carr, Ann Swallow, Julie Fotos, Robert Condon, Ellen DeRiso and Jacky Grossman.

Mario: To my intimate brands: Laura Monardo, Isabella Natarelli, Olivia Natarelli, Vittoria Natarelli, Gentile Natarelli, Anna Provenzano, Cathie Evans, Fausto Natarelli, Lou Natarelli, Lucia Monardo, Egidio Monardo, Guspare Provenzano, John Evans, Luisa Natarelli, Joanne Natarelli, Anna Rossetti, John Rossetti, Carmen Lago, George Lago, Gabriel D'Andrea, Anna D'Andrea, Francesco Provenzano, Matthew Rossetti, Christina Natarelli, Joe Evans, Vittoria Natarelli, Sarah Rossetti, Jim Evans, Grace Natarelli, Rose Natarelli, Elisa Natarelli, Steve Evans, Mark Lago, Alex Lago, Leo D'Andrea, Lucio Zoppi and Family.

To our clients and business partners who have inspired us the most

Atif Abdulmalik, HE Mommad Alabbar, Wahid Attalla, Rashid Al Malik, Marwan Al Serkhal, Khalid Al Zarooni, Jonathan Bell, Kati Bergou, HE Sultan bin Sulayem, Tammy Burke, Paige Costigan, Juan Pablo De Valle, Danah Ditzig, Bill Hays, Jeff Hirsch, Simon Horgan, David Jackson, Elaine Jones, Peter Krauss, Suzanne Lavin, Jazia Mohammed, Hamza Mustafa, Andrea Prochniak, Richard Rubenstein, Saeed Ahmed Saeed, David Spencer, Paul Taubman.

Mario Natarelli

Mario is the Managing Partner at MBLM in New York and an established marketing leader to executives and their companies. Over the past 20 years, Mario has helped companies of every size and type, working across the globe to transform, align and manage their brands to deliver growth and value. Prior to MBLM, Mario was the CEO of FutureBrand North America and Middle East and was the co-founder of HyperMedia. Mario is a graduate architect with a degree from the University of Toronto.

Rina Plapler

Rina is a Partner at MBLM and has built brands for over 20 years. She leads strategy at MBLM in New York and has held executive positions at FutureBrand and Gormley & Partners. Rina has worked with B2B, B2C and B2G companies and has extensive strategy experience across a variety of industries including financial services, tourism, health care, technology and telecommunications. She was the creator of FutureBrand's Country Brand Index and MBLM's Brand Intimacy Study. Rina has degrees from McGill and Harvard Universities.

INDEX